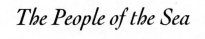

The People of the Sea

Books by David Thomson

The People of the Sea
Daniel, *a novel*
Break in the Sun, *a novel*
The Leaping Hare, *with George Ewart Evans*
Woodbrook
In Camden Town
Dandiprat's Days, *a novel*
Nairn in Darkness and Light

The Irish Journals of Elizabeth Smith, 1840–1850
A selection, edited with Moyra McGusty

Danny Fox
Danny Fox Meets a Stranger
Danny Fox at the Palace
Ronan and Other Stories

The People of the Sea

A Journey in Search of the Seal Legend

David Thomson

Introduction by Seamus Heaney

Decorations by Jonathan Heale

COUNTERPOINT

WASHINGTON, D.C.

First published in Great Britain by Turnstile Press Ltd in 1954.
Revised editions 1965 and 1980.
First Counterpoint hardcover edition 2000.
First Counterpoint paperback edition 2002.

Library of Congress Cataloging-in-Publication Data
Thomson, David, 1914-1988
The people of the sea : a journey in search of the seal
legend / David Thomson ; introduced by Seamus Heaney.
p. cm.
First published in 1954.
ISBN 1-58243-184-1 (alk. paper)
1. Seals (Animals)—Folklore. I. Title.
GR730.S4 T47 2000
398.24'52979—dc21   00-055515

Printed in the United States of America on acid-free paper that meets
the American National Standards Institute z39-48 Standard

COUNTERPOINT
P.O. Box 65793
Washington, DC 20035-5793

Counterpoint is a member of the Perseus Books Group.

To Martina

Contents

Introduction *by Seamus Heaney*   xiii

Foreword *by David Thomson*   xxi

The People of the Sea   3

The Music of the Seals   199

Acknowledgments   211

"I am a man upo' the land,
I am a selchie in the sea."

Introduction

"It canna be true," says Osie, the Orkney crofter who appears in Chapter 7 of this memorable book, "but there was supposed to be a creature in the water for every one on land." And a moment later, insisting again "This canna be true," he tells the author a story about a stranger cow that came up from the sea and installed herself in a byre on the land. "And she had grand calves. But I forget, now, was it a seal or another cow came years after to the door o' the byre . . . and the cow went away to the sea again." And then comes the clinching cadence: "An old woman told me yon," said Osie. "Well, there was supposed to be cows and sheep and every animal there. But the seals were the people o' the sea."

In the presence of such alluring inventions and such a credible voice, there's hardly any need for commentary. Talk of the willing suspension of disbelief, of the salubrious effect of imaginative narrative, characterizations of the mental habits of pre-industrial societies, conjectures about how the sociological facts got displaced in earlier days into the parallel universe of the mythological—all this seems to lead in the wrong direction. David Thomson's book is luminously its own thing; it had its origins in one man's rambles round the highlands and islands of Scotland and the west coast of Ireland, in search of stories and folklore surrounding the "selchie" or gray Atlantic seal. It was written at a great moment in the history of radio, during the 1940s and 1950s, when the BBC employed poets and

writers to record and collect oral material and—most important—
gave them permission to re-create it in a new artistic form. Conse-
quently it survives not as a period piece but as a poetic achievement,
one of whose works written by "a man speaking to men: a man, it
is true, endued with more lively sensibility, more enthusiasm and
tenderness, who has a greater knowledge of human nature, and a
more comprehensive soul, than are supposed to be common among
mankind . . . "

William Wordsworth's definition of a poet, which I have just
quoted, seems an appropriate characterization of the man who
wrote *The People of the Sea.* Indeed, what kept coming to mind as I
re-read the book was Wordsworth's poem "The Solitary Reaper."
One of the most haunting lyrics in the English language, this too
was written after a tour in Scotland and is about the experience of
listening to a local woman express herself unforgettably in her native
Gaelic. The sight of women working in the harvest fields must have
been a common one at the time, but interestingly enough, the poet
found his immediate inspiration in the manuscript of a book by his
friend Thomas Wilkinson: "Passed by a Female who was reaping
alone, she sung in Erse as she bended over her sickle, the sweetest
human voice I ever heard. Her strains were tenderly melancholy,
and felt delicious long after they were heard no more." Wordsworth's final stanza uses some of Wilkinson's exact words, but what
was notation in the prose becomes incantation in the poem:

> Whate'er the theme, the Maiden sang
> As if her song could have no ending;
> I saw her singing at her work,
> And o'er the sickle bending;—
> I listened, motionless and still;
> And, as I mounted up the hill,
> The music in my heart I bore,
> Long after it was heard no more.

This famous stanza is like a spell that keeps time, in two senses: it
keeps the metrical beat of the octosyllabic line, and it also manages
to shift into the eternal present of song-time an incident that might

otherwise have remained part of the accidental record. When Wordsworth's lines are repeated, the reader or listener re-enters the prolonged trance that the first listener experienced; "the Maiden" still sings "as if her song could have no ending" because of the entrancing, prolonging power of the rhymes and cadences. The chance words of Thomas Wilkinson's *Tour of Scotland* have been magicked into the domain of the eternally recurrent, the once-upon-a-time world of story, where the strains of "no ending" and "still" and "more" echo and overflow above the brim of the usual.

The transformations and transports that Wordsworth effects in verse in "The Solitary Reaper," David Thomson manages to encompass in the prose—narrative, lyrical, dramatic—of *The People of the Sea*. Here too, what was heard in the "chaunt" of the storyteller gets fixed on the page, only to rise in all its formality and down-to-earthness at each re-reading. Notations of the author's different tours of Scotland (and of Ireland) have been re-imagined and re-presented in an idiom that makes the reader a kind of dual citizen, at once the inhabitant of a poetically beguiling world of pure story and of a realistically documented world of fishermen and crofters. In these pages, by performing the task of the historian he was trained to be and that of the artist he was born to become, David Thomson is answering the two calls that reality made upon him. He envisages even as he records, with the result that librarians are probably hard put to find an exact category for the book: it has elements of both "fiction" and "nonfiction." Readers, on the other hand, will be carried away on the successive waves of pleasure, as the here-and-nowness of the people and scenes evoked by the author gives way to there-and-thenness of the stories they narrate.

David Thomson's achievement is pre-eminently stylistic; his writing combines a feel for the "this-worldness" of his characters' lives with an understanding of the "otherworldness" they can credit in their stories. Which is a way of saying that the stylistic achievement depends upon a deep imaginative sympathy. What could have been a matter of field work being written up into a casebook becomes a matter of memory and its contents being liberated into a new and transfigured pattern. The book recovers and revives the old trope of human beings as creatures dwelling in a middle state, caught between the worlds of the angels and the animals; it is obviously an archive of lore about the seal, and obliquely an account of traditional cultures on the verge of dissolution, but at the mythic level it presents us with an image of ourselves in those amphibians we have evolved from, all of us (to quote Wordsworth again) "inmates of this active universe."

What delights is the absence of nostalgia. Even as the men in a cabin give themselves up to an eerie tale of child-kidnap by a seal, one of them is talking about remedies for the warble-fly: "I tried motor oil and sulfur powder mixed." Even as a storyteller invokes the ancient glamour of the Celtic *ceo draíochta,* he resolutely demystifies it: "So the seal set up a magic fog, or what is called in modern parlance a smoke screen . . ." And yet, for all the up-to-dateness of the idiom, the fundamental understanding of these characters is shaped by what the poet Edwin Muir once termed "that long lost, archaic companionship" between human beings and the creatures. Plainly, memorably, repeatedly, instances of this old eye-to-eye and breath-to-breath closeness between living things appear in the narrative. Michael the Ferryman judges the strength of the current he is rowing into by watching the toils of the big seal in heavy water adjacent to the boat; a child escaped from drowning is warmed back to consciousness in a "Black House" in South Uist between the generous bodies of two cows; on Papa Stour in Shetland, in an old cowshed, the author himself gradually attains a state of almost animal consciousness:

> I heard a raven croak twice. I felt the autumn coldly on my face, but because this old cowshed had been lately used for dipping sheep there was a smell of dung as though the warm life of the farm lingered on.

Edwin Muir's sense of the need for a renewed covenant with all life and a respect for its sacredness was inspired directly by the shadow of nuclear destruction that loomed over the 1950s. It may be pushing things to suggest that David Thomson's book was equally prompted by the prevailing mood, but it is no exaggeration to say that it continues to present itself to the understanding as an elegy for certain salvific elements which "progress" and modernity were bound to destroy.

The sweetness and intimacy of David Thomson's imagination mean that he is able to bring us very close to that vanished world. His complete at-homeness in the crofts and cabins and "Black Houses" he entered, his ability to be all ear and eye, allow the reader access to the otherness of the minds and manners of those he met. Total respect, intuitive understanding, perfect grace and perfect pitch— possessed of such gifts, he was never regarded as an intruder. The naturalness of his presence seems always to have made up for its unexpectedness; he arrived into other people's lives as simply and mysteriously as Michael the Ferryman arrived into his:

> I stopped to look at a cairn of stones by the roadside. Out of a hole in the ground about fifty yards away, where he was cutting turf, a man came slowly to me.
> "It's a nice day," I said.
> "It is grand drying weather, thanks be to God."

In this exchange, the one tiny variation that the Mayo man plays on the author's opening greeting is a guarantee of the complete delicacy and accuracy of David Thomson's ear. The replacement of "It's" by "It is" indicates the different measure and ever so slight caution of the Irish voice in the English tongue, and reveals in detail the overall trustworthiness of this writing. Little touches carry us at one time out into the exposed spaces of the elemental world, as when he talks of Shetland sheep, "their horns warm to touch in the rain"; at another time, a whole culture of human endurance is conjured up in a single observation, as when the young Ronald Iain Finlay remembers coming to in his mother's arms. His father had been drowned and the boy had been washed ashore: "My mother was weeping again, and I clung to the warmth of her, watching the faces about us, and the faces were steady." That steadiness reminds me of Homer's Odysseus bearing up, "his eyelids steady as wrinkled horn or iron," listening *incognito* while the bard Demodicus recites the tale of Troy.

And yet for all the Homeric somberness underlying the attitude of the characters, what is constantly to the fore in the writing is something more gamboling, something more like Arion escaping on the dolphin's back. It is the benignity and essential justice of the relations pertaining between the people of the land and the people of the sea that give these stories an irresistible holistic beauty. Mother seals that suckle human infants, gentlemen seals that provide seal-back rides to the November fair and then go for a drink afterward, wounded seals that require the hand that cut them open to close them up again, lover seals that arrive "at the seventh stream" to meet the yearning young wife—"and it wasna for good they met so often"—these are not escapist fantasies but a form of poetry, especially if we think of poetry in terms of its definition as a dream dreamt in the presence of reason.

I was lucky enough to get to know David Thomson and his wife, Martina, twenty years after the publication of *The People of the Sea*. *Woodbrook* (1974), a book that was at once an erotic idyll and a work of historical reconstruction, had just appeared and was making a great stir. It told of David's arrival in Ireland in the 1930s as tutor to the young daughter of an Anglo-Irish family in County Roscommon, and through that story contrived also to tell the story of other realities—social, cultural, historical and political—that had been central to Irish life for centuries. Again, this was a version of pastoral, the world regarded through an artfully innocent eye, one that thereby revealed all the more lucidly rights and wrongs, hurts and beauties, usually taken for granted. A result of its success was the increased frequency of the Thomsons' visits to Dublin and other parts of the country, and the opportunity to become friends. By the time of David's death in 1988, the writer whom I had first got to know in print as the co-author (with George Ewart Evans) of another classic beast-book, *The Leaping Hare* (1972), had published two further books of autobiography, *In Camden Town* (1983) and *Nairn in Darkness and Light* (1987), work where he followed his own creative, truth-telling bent with characteristic unpredictability and sprightliness.

Nairn in Darkness and Light takes him back to the house he calls Tigh na Rosan in the first chapter of *The People of the Sea,* and in the later book he re-creates the Edwardian order of life that reigned there for a few years after the First World War. As the son of a father who had served in the Indian Army and had been wounded in the trenches, David was sprung from that socially privileged world, but at the age of eleven what might have been an education and a career typical of one of his class was interrupted. Because of an injury to his eye, which would drastically impair his sight for years to come, his parents sent him north out of England to the large, sea-lit security of his grandparents' home, and it was because of the uncanny purity of his account of that place, and of the life he lived in it, that I found myself one summer night a few years after David's death, on the pier at Nairn.

Behind me, the big house he had dwelt in was now a hotel, but out beyond, the Moray Firth still clucked at the pier-head and glimmered like cloudy pewter as far as the horizon. Then suddenly in the early dark the strollers were murmuring and halting, hands were pointing toward an agitation in the water farther out. I heard the word "dolphins." There was a perceptible flitter and rollick in the dark offing, and all through my body a tremor of joy: I couldn't help imagining our friend in his other world, out there astride the dolphin's back, scanning the waves for a selchie, haring it for all he was worth toward the open sea.

Seamus Heaney
September 1999

Foreword

When I arrived in Ireland a year or two ago on my way to revisit some of the seal places of the West, a Dublin friend told me that Fitzwilliam Square had just been opened as a public park. "Go and see it," he said, "before the gardeners get in with their tulips." From the top of a hillock I could only just see the houses through a gap between beautifully untended trees. The grass had been mown but was more like a meadow than a lawn, and wild flowers and birds were plentiful. I had not seen much of the West of Ireland since I began to write this book nearly thirty years before and, imagining many changes, I feared that the cultural gardeners might have reached it with concrete symmetry at their heels. That has not happened, but perhaps it is true that in the late 1940s, when I first explored the western fringe of Europe from the Shetland Islands to the coast of Kerry, I came only just in time to hear the last remnants of pre-Christian culture.

Even in those years young people who loved and sang the old songs became uneasy when their parents began to tell traditional stories such as those recorded in this book, just as children do if you recite their infant sayings. The link with their forefathers, the passing on of history, genealogy, legend and belief by word of mouth, was beginning to weaken even then, as skills such as rope-making and thatching are weakening now. And now, so far as I can perceive, there remains with the exception of religion and language no direct cultural link with the past. Only traditional music has survived and been revived. New generations of children learn to play the pipes or fiddle at school. They love the old songs and sing them but usually learn from recordings, which, I am told, creates a uniformity unknown to their grandparents, who never sang the same song in the same way twice. Narrative is no longer heard and no longer passes from father to son. I came to the seal places during the years of transition and knew even then that contact with industrialized society had begun to make some storytellers shy of expressing themselves to their own children. They found more acceptable listeners among strangers, and strangers were few; the absence of physical comfort, the hard weather, scanty food and lack of transport kept holidaymakers away.

Shyness toward me as a stranger affected this book in only one way. Many people asked me not to mention them by name in print, and often they were reluctant to tell a story until I promised to disguise the names of families mentioned in it, and even the names of some places. I regret this but have kept my promise. I believe that the very request meant more than a normal misgiving about betraying family secrets, that it was one sign of changing attitudes, for many of the older storytellers gave real names freely. It was their younger friends who held them back—those who were beginning to feel self-conscious about the old tradition. But in the conversation that often followed a story, those younger people showed no fear. They spoke, for example, of intuitive perception such as second sight without any doubt at all.

I have changed too, of course. When I first heard the stories I was enlightened in a simple way. I liked them for themselves alone, as I hope most readers will. Since then I have read analyses and interpretations, and learned that the motifs of the seal occur in other settings, with other animals as a central figure, all over the world. Individuals have seen religious symbolism in them. Others have pointed to their psychological significance. This has not spoiled my first enjoyment. It has enhanced it. For all great storytelling, spoken or written, contains layer upon layer of meaning, and the older you grow, the more you experience actual and imaginative life, the deeper you are drawn.

As to the seals themselves, no scientific study can dissolve their mystery. Land animals may play their roles in legend, but none, not even the hare, has such a dream-like effect on the human mind; and so, though many creatures share with them a place in our unconscious mind, a part in ancient narrative, the seal legend is unique. Walk on their lonely beaches, climb on to their rocks with the knowledge that the sea before you stretches unbroken to America, that for thousands of years people believed what you now feel—that you are at the uttermost edge of the earth—and when all is quiet except for waves and sea birds, you hear an old man gasp. You turn toward the sound. It is a seal that has broken the surface of the water to take a breath, and, very often, seeing you it will raise its whole torso and stare back at you to assess the danger, or from curiosity—then disappear silently. And watching the rocks for them, who like to bask in the sun, you will think there are none until one notices your presence and there is a splash and you see what you thought was a rock splash into the sea. More splashes as the others follow; they usually come on land in fours or fives. As a South Uist man told me on my last visit to the island in 1979, "When you look at the rocks, you will think there are no seals, but the seals are there." A young man said, "They are plentiful. We don't interfere with them. We leave them alone."

Everywhere where the gray Atlantic seal has lived for generations places are named after them: Seal Bay, Seal Strand, Seal Skerries or Rocks, the Beach of Seals, the Seal Place. And on all my return journeys I found the wildness of such places untamed. The people who have lived beside them for generations live a little bit more comfortably than did their parents and grandparents who gave me the substance of this book; most of their houses are supplied with tap water and all except a very few have electricity from hydro-electric schemes. Electricity led to television, which has completely altered the way in which they spend their leisure. Even those who have no set are affected by the piecemeal scraps that issue from it, the sudden spurts of fun and information soon forgotten that have disturbed the surface of a steady ancient stream. But nothing has changed the nature of the people so much praised by travelers in Ireland as early as the seventeenth century and ever since, in Scotland by Defoe and even Dr. Johnson. They are a serious people, in the sense the French use the word *sérieux*. They are honorable, considerate, and gentle in manner. Where else would a stranger find a ferryman who charged his passengers half fare because sea mist had kept them waiting twenty-four hours? That happened to me at Ludag, on the island on South Uist, in 1979, on my way to Barra. I had had to return to my lodgings a mile away and the crofter's wife did not want to charge me the extra night. "But you did not intend to stay," she said.

There are in most of the seal places more people than there were in the two decades after the war. New industries and quicker transport have given the young a chance to work at a distance and live at home, and this together with modern household equipment, which includes the TV set, has brought many back or made them stay.

"Say not thou," said Ecclesiastes the preacher, "what is the cause that former days were better than these?" And elsewhere he said, "One generation passeth away and another generation cometh: but the earth abideth for ever . . . All the rivers run into the sea; yet the sea is not full; unto the place from whence the rivers come, thither they return again."

David Thomson
July 1979

The People of the Sea

OF ALL THE HOUSES THAT I REMEMBER WITH LOVE the house called Tigh na Rosan is the sweetest smelling and the brightest. That is to say it is the best of the clean and ordered houses I have lived in. There have been houses that gave by their straw furniture and smells and tattered wallpaper a feeling of ease and warmth unknown to Tigh na Rosan, houses where volunteers were asked for during supper, when it rained, to fetch another jam pot to catch a new drip from the ceiling, houses that smelt of bats and mice, houses that made your eyes smart for the first three weeks because the nests of jackdaws in the chimney sent the smoke back into the rooms, houses that smelt of tar and fish, houses too dark to read in, or too bare and hard to sit down in, and these in their way I have loved more. But of clean and moneyed houses Tigh na Rosan is the best.

It is built of granite by the sea, on the northern part of the east coast of Scotland, in a hard, small town called Nairn, which on fine days lies opposite the blue cliffs of Cromarty and on gray days looks out at a rigid black skyline, very close and broken in the middle by a gap called Cromarty Firth.

The drawing room of Tigh na Rosan looks out in this direction across a lawn through wide, high windows. In winter hail and wind beat on it from the north and east. In summer the sun slants across the garden, but the drawing room smells of roses and of potpourri and is always cool. In the drawing room you do not forget about the sea.

I first went there with my sisters and my mother and father when I was about five. I got to know the drawing room well, because it had in it an ostrich egg, a large stuffed bird that was gray and scraggy, and a little Indian man who stood on a pedestal on the piano and would not fall off even if you laid him on his side to start him rocking. But I thought a lot more of the pantry, where there was black powder and a polishing machine with a curved handle and a slot for every size of knife. From the pantry and the drawing room you could see the sea and often you could hear it. It was in the drawing room that I heard La speak about Mrs. Carnoustie and it was in the pantry later that I questioned Mina about Mrs. Carnoustie's legs.

La was my mother's cousin. From my place by the windowsill where I was trying to make a red ladybird climb on to a leaf, I heard her say that Mrs. Carnoustie was deformed. My mother could not remember that, and La screamed with laughter.

"Do you mean she was a hunchback?" I said.

And La said, "No. Her back was all right—a bit round, that's all. She was round all over, and fat. She was very smooth and slippery looking."

"Did she have an iron boot?"

"No. But she couldn't walk very well. Her legs were like flippers."

"That's absurd, La," said my mother.

"You must remember. You must. I remember her arms too. It's perfectly true. They only came down a little below where the elbows should be and they were supposed to be flattish, but you never really saw them because she wore big sleeves, big full ones, and I think they were sewn up at the ends. But they looked flattish, like flippers, and she held them against her sides or across her chest and she moved them rather awkwardly. But you could never see her legs. We always wanted to. We wanted to see her in her bath and of course we couldn't, and it was terrible, I remember, never being able to know, and of course we couldn't ask her or anyone else really—anyway we couldn't get proper answers from anyone. And, you see, she was always in the same kind of dress—a long, long gray shiny dress, silk I think, that fastened at the neck with a close collar and came right down to the ground and hid everything."

"Everybody's dresses came right down to the ground," said my mother.

"Not as much as hers did, and she was very round and bulged out in the dress in kind of crinkles. And her face was round and plump too, with a small nose sort of flattened and a big wide sort of mouth. And I think she had a kind of moustache."

"I remember the moustache," said my mother. "Or was it that other woman who had a moustache?"

"It was Mrs. Carnoustie. It must have been Mrs. Carnoustie. I remember everything about her. She had black shiny hair—lots of it, but it was close on her head and very smooth. She was smooth looking, all over. And she had brown eyes." La stopped and I ignored the ladybird.

I said, "How did she drink her tea?"

"What?"

"If her sleeves were sewn up she couldn't have lifted a cup."

"I think she could clutch things in an awkward sort of way with both arms."

"Then it would spill!"

"No it wouldn't," said my mother. "You could hold it with two hands, as though you had mittens on. I don't mean mittens. I mean those gloves without fingers."

"Yes, you could," I said. "Only it would be difficult writing letters after Christmas."

"I don't suppose she bothered much. Mr. Carnoustie used to do nearly everything for her."

"Did he have his sleeves sewn up?"

"Oh no. He was an ordinary man. He had been married before to quite an ordinary woman, everybody said, but after she died he went away for a long time, and when he came back he bought another house near us and he got married to this strange woman. Her eyes were very queer."

"Why?"

"They were very big. Enormous. And brown."

"Were they as big as a horse's eyes?"

"They must have been as big as a seal's eyes!"

"Why?"

"Because she was supposed to be a seal."

"Why was she?"

"People said her mother was a seal. They said her father had met a woman wandering about on the beach somewhere on the west coast, and he got married to this woman. But people said the woman was really a seal disguised as a woman. And so when they had a baby it turned out to be half a seal and it grew up to be Mrs. Carnoustie."

I said, "Did you say she couldn't walk?"

"She could get about all right. But it was slow. We thought she hadn't really got two legs under her dress just a sort of continuation of her body and two flat feet sticking out sideways."

"I bet she could swim," I said. And I swam on my stomach on the carpet, making a noise like the seal I had seen at a circus.

"She wasn't allowed to swim," said La.

"Why?"

"I don't know why. But I know we did ask her once, just to see what she'd say. And she said Mr. Carnoustie didn't like bathing. We wanted her to go into the sea, because then she would have had to take her long dress off."

I now think that Mina was the mildest and kindest and probably the weakest woman in the world. She was our nurse at that time and we tormented her, but after she was married to a sweetshop man we used often to visit her in her house and then we knew how fond of her we were. She died much too young of a tumor on the brain.

I went into the pantry through the green baize door that opened both ways without a latch and she was standing with her back to me washing something in the sink. Her hair was done up in a thick sleek bun. It was black and shining, covering her temples and her ears and neck. My mother had told me that when she let it down it was so long that she could sit on it. As a greeting she said, "Now!" when she heard me, but she did not look round, so I stood with my back to the door and surveyed her. Her heels were together, and her feet stuck out sideways in black low-heeled shoes. I went up and banged her tentatively behind the knees. She said "Now!" again, this time as a warning. I banged the calves of her legs, trying to hit them in the middle to see if they were joined, and she said gently, spacing out the words in her slow Highland way, "No, dearie, no. Don't do that!" which made me laugh, because it was usually to my sister Joan she spoke in those words with what she thought was severity. Her mild "No, Cho-an, dearie, don't do that" had become a catchword with us. So I laughed and tapped her ankles with my boot.

"Have you got legs like Mrs. Carnoustie?"

"Who might Mrs. Carnoustie be?"

"She's a seal in a long dress and she's got flippers for legs."

"Dear me, she must be one of the selchie folk, so."

"Have you ever seen one?"

"No, dearie, no. It's nothing but an old wifie's tale."

"Is La an old wifie?"

"Indeed, how dare you say such things of Miss Chalmers."

"Well, she saw Mrs. Carnoustie swimming in the bath like a seal. Mrs. Carnoustie turned on the water, took off all her clothes and got in and La saw her legs—kind of all in one with two flat feet sticking out sideways like yours. Mrs. Carnoustie swam like this." I showed her and barked like the seal in the circus.

"I never heard a selchie make a noise like that. It's more like a dog."

"Is a selchie the same as a seal?"

"She's a big gray seal. She makes a moaning sound and she would put the heart across you with her wailing in the night."

"Will I see a selchie if I go to the beach?"

"There's no selchies here at Nairn. You'd only see Tangies here, and Tangies are smaller and quite ordinary seals. They don't come ashore to live like people. And they don't care for music in the same way. Of course, there's no truth in those tales."

"Mina?"

"Yes, dearie."

"Grandma says your brains are made of hair."

"Well, if Mrs. Finlay says so it must be true."

I learned to read at Miss Squair's, and then we left Nairn for Derbyshire, for one of the ramshackle houses away from the sea where our lives were filled with a fox terrier called Kuti and a young wounded crow that Joan had rescued from some boys. Kuti lived with us for twelve years. Jim Crow lived for two years and a bit, partly in the house and partly on the top of a tall tree where he kept a lookout for my mother and would if he felt like it fly down and perch on her hat as she rode past on her bicycle. He died at about the age of two when I was seven.

My imagination while we lived inland was inspired by fire engines, which were pulled at the gallop by horses and which flung behind them a stream of red coals; by the contemplation of sun-baked cowpats; and by the awful thought of wolves. I suppose most children are uncertain whether to feel relieved or disappointed when they first find out that wolves no longer live wild in England. Into my heart the thought of the wolf struck terror and romance. Old shepherds of the Bible, old shepherds of the Scottish Highlands, Mina's home, the fierce and dashing chases through the Russian steppes, where desperate drivers cut the traces of one horse and sacrificed it to gain time, the lonely caves on mountain tops, the blackness of the forests, fear, curiosity, the terrifying desire to witness death—these dreams and a hankering for wild places set the wolf before me like a stark silhouette.

The thought of the seal was softer, but the mystery was the same. I had never seen one, but when I went back to Nairn they lived near me, and the country people with whom I spent a lot of time at the age of eleven were in touch with them. The salmon fishermen who lived throughout the summer in a tarred bothy on the deserted shore talked often of them, of how they would damage the nets and destroy the salmon—not in hunger but in play. Bob MacDonald showed me three big salmon lying dead, each with a bite taken out of its neck.

"They live like toffs," he told me. "Nothing is good for them, only the tenderest part of the flesh. And often times they kill for the sake of killing—like a cat with mice. And one of them will do a hundred pounds of damage to the nets in a night." He would follow such talk with stories that turned my stomach, describing in horrid detail the brutal revenge that he and his mates had taken on the individual seals they rarely caught. And if Douglas Macrae, the oldest of the fishermen, was there when these stories were told, he would look blank while the others laughed. "He believes in the old wifie's tales," Bob would whisper to me. "He's from the West." And asking no questions I gradually learned to associate the death of a seal with the death of the albatross in "The Ancient Mariner," which we had learned by heart at school.

At this time in Nairn, living with my aunt and grandmother at Tigh na Rosan, I visited at various hours of the day the two men who had undertaken to teach me—a tall, pale minister of the Episcopal Church, and a retired schoolmaster who had kindly, sun-reddened cheeks; but most of my time, from six o'clock in the morning, when I met Bob's father, Duncan MacDonald, and drove the milk cart for him, till four or five in the evening, when I fed the cart horses, was spent working in, or playing at, or dreaming of Sandwood Farm. My grandmother apologized daily to these men and their wives for the smell of cow dung, which she knew so well from my boots.

Tigh na Rosan had ceased to cause me surprise. Romance was made of the shadows and the wooden posts, the chains and buckets, the dark shapes hanging from the rafters, the bins of brown linseed cake, the dung and straw and hay, the steamy warmth, soft flanks and bony hips, warm udders, some with teats that were good to touch, some scabby or misshapen, the taste of the hot froth of new milk, the slow eyes of cattle and horses, the rhythmic munching, the coughing and the shuffling of the byre and stable. Death was only real at the gates of the shambles at Nairn, or by the strawstack when Bob had his hand round the throat of a cockerel. Violence was real in the muddy lane behind Trades Park where the black bull mounted a cow and I was planted with a stick to bar their way from the main road. Birth became real by the light of a hurricane lamp, while a cow moaned and bellowed as three men pulled the calf from her, leaning back with all their strength on a rope, as at a tug-of-war. The men who did this were part of a society that I feared and loved. I was happy with them often. Their activities and the places where they worked excited my mind and drew me into action, but because of Tigh na Rosan I could never be one of them and could never get rid of the fear. I wanted to be with the women who made crowdie and huge girdle scones in the farmhouse, with the dustmen whose cart I tracked beyond the harbor to the waste by the sea where they tipped their load and sorted it unwatched, with the old leather-faced woman alone in her tarred hovel on the carse, or with the pig-man two miles from her by himself with his ponies and pigs. When I drove the milk in the early morning from house to house through the narrow lanes of the fishertown, filling jugs on the doorsteps beside black huts where the herrings were smoked, and when I rattled up the High Street with my empty cans at too fast a trot, I felt for an hour or two that I was one of them. Driving the farm cart on the long, slow road to the distillery near Cawdor, I was one of them again. But Tigh na Rosan and the men who taught me came in between. And when I reached the distillery and waited with the other carts to be loaded with hot draff, my accent betrayed me and I was ashamed.

I suppose it is not an unusual thing to live two lives in that sense. Perhaps many children divide their attention between the people and animals that are familiar and near and those that are unapproachable, clouded with mysteries and dreaming fear. With me it was so. I liked well enough my aunt and grandmother and their friends who lived near Tigh na Rosan in what the shopkeepers liked to call "the west end" of Nairn. Tigh na Rosan itself with its clarity and precision, with the way it had of tying one's mind to the pleasant aspects of the past, with its windows looking and its garden gate opening toward sea and sand that were not muddled, must have given the people who lived in it a sense of security of which they were not conscious, and a routine whose value I at least saw only after I had lost it. This house and its people, and by slower stages even the farm animals, shed their enchantment as they drew close. The dustmen and the fishermen and farmers could not draw close. Nor could the wolves and the seals.

Next door to Sandwood Farm there was a big house called Sandwood. The farm I suppose had belonged to it in the days when gentlemen farmers flourished near the Moray Firth, but now the house belonged to my uncle, a businessman who had a daughter called Patsy a few years younger than I. It was the summer time. It was somebody's birthday, I think—Patsy's probably—and as the shadows of the guests and trees stretched thin and long in the evening sun there was a dwarf like a witch in a homemade booth. Although I knew that the witch's feet, which fidgeted and stamped as she stood on the table on a level with my shoulders, were really my mother's hands concealed in black stockings and old shoes like slugs, and that the rest of the shortened body, the arms that could touch her ankles without stretching, her contorted voice and face, half hidden, half muffled behind a veil with spiders on it, was really made up of Mina's Miss Chalmers—my mother's mysterious and lovable cousin La—I was afraid. The dwarf witch gave presents to me and to my cousin Patsy.

Patsy had black, shining hair; her face, neck and arms were the color of thick cream, and every now and then I was in love with her secretly. By looking in the prayer book of the Episcopal Church of Scotland, which was something like the Church of England, except that, as I gathered from the minister who taught me, it regarded the Archbishop of Canterbury with the same distrust as most Protestants allow to the Pope, I had found out that cousins were permitted to marry.

In the garden under the fir trees there were raspberries and cream and cakes and milk and lemonade. There were musical chairs and tig and a child's version without the kissing of "Here we go gathering nuts and may," and suddenly I saw outside myself that everyone was laughing, that everyone was happy, including me. And there were chocolate biscuits and cream cookies and everything was as good as it ever had been or could be. One of the grown-up people began to organize my favorite game, which we called "French and English," a mock fight with lines like the battle lines in the books I then read, such as *Brigadier Gerard*. I was chosen for the French side—the only side that pleased me. Patsy was on my side. I could defend, or pretend to defend, her. The sun shone sideways through the trees, and the sky between the pine needles overhead was blue. My sister Joan was on my side too, and the boy who lived at Clach na Mara was one of those against us. Life on this earth at that moment was arranged like heaven.

There is a time during the plans for "French and English" when the opposing armies are mixed together talking and unsorted. Nobody would notice one who disappeared. At the height of interest and bright anticipation I chose this moment to slink out. I went through the darkness of the pinewood to the broken gate that used to open on to the stackyard of Sandwood Farm. The old farmer, Duncan, was there beyond the gate with four of his sons and two of his daughters building the first of the oatstacks alongside the hay. Crouching out of sight, I watched them. They made jokes and laughed. I crawled away from them behind the fence. Scratching my knees on the dead twigs that lay on the ground, I crawled till I knew I was out of sight of the farmyard and the party. Then I ran down across two fields toward the sea. I ran to the beach. Then I ran to the west, away from Nairn, away from Tigh na Rosan.

I stopped beside a whin bush and sat down. I played a solitary game of marbles in the sand with rabbit droppings hardened by the sun and I found a dead rabbit with a bloody hole on the nape of its neck which I knew had been made by a stoat. Then I walked on.

The sand was on my right, ribbed by the tide, which had gone out, then the sea with calm ripples shaped the same, and further to my right, the cliffs of Cromarty mottled black and blue by the fine evening. The gap where the Firth lay was in a new place now, and looked unlike the place one saw from Tigh na Rosan. And the sea was flat, with no boats. The carse was flat too, and in the west ahead of me a black mass of cloud began to reduce the sunset to a block like the door of a furnace. I tied my sandshoes by their laces to my belt and walked along.

The carse, as it is called in Scotland, is a level strip of land by the sea, usually uncultivated, scattered with whin bushes and broom and clothed rather patchily with short grass cut close by the wind or cropped by sheep—I am not sure which. I hardly ever saw anything alive on the carse. Perhaps one man in the distance for a moment, perhaps four or five black-faced sheep, a lark rising rarely, curlews and plovers in the air; but on the ground I can remember only corpses and white skeletons and dead wood bleached like bone. The only house ahead of me now was the bothy where the salmon fishermen lived during the week. It would be empty now, I thought, because it was Saturday night.

The bothy was a low hut built of tarred sleepers and driftwood and roofed with sods of grass. A fine crop of wild flowers grew on the roof. The window was cracked and webbed over by spiders and there was a smell of tar and rotting fish. I looked in through the window, but could see nothing in the darkness but a small cracked mirror with a safety razor lying on it. I went cautiously to the door and pushed it open.

One shaft of dusty light stretched from the little window to the corner farthest from me, but all I could see from the door into the darkness were the ends of three wooden bunks built one above the other against the wall. There was a torn towel hanging from a nail and a picture of a naked woman hanging sideways from a pin. I imagined for a moment as I held my breath that there was someone in the room and drew back, pulling the door behind me inch by inch. After a few minutes, while I stood on the white pebbles watching the cloud grow wider and the evening darker, a struggle between fear and curiosity, between the fear of being caught in a place which I had no right to enter and the fear I had of giving in to fear, drove me in to the bothy again. I thought I might find a candle and matches, climb up to the top bunk and lie there to find out what it felt like to sleep without sheets away from Tigh na Rosan, on the carse alone. The beds at Sandwood Farm had no sheets on them. I had made sure of that.

Inside the hut it was like night by now and the smell of fish was strong. I went step by step silently across the wooden floor. And then I put my foot in something wet and warm.

I gasped, gulped air back down my throat and clenched my teeth into the back of my hand, and stood terrified on one foot, quickly thinking where it would be safe to put the other. I tried it behind me; a step back, something moved and I felt an old man's hairy head against my ankle; to the side and I was in the sticky stuff again. I leapt to the table by the window and sat on it. The mirror and the razor clattered down. I screamed and put both hands over my eyes. I heard heavy breathing. The smell of fish grew worse and the bothy hotter. My mouth was full of spittle. I was sick between my legs on to the floor.

A minute or an hour later I was still on the table when I heard the pebbles crunch outside and looking up saw the outline of a man in the doorway, holding in his arms a bundle of driftwood.

"Who is that there?" he said.

"It's me," I said.

"You're welcome," he said.

"I've been sick," I said, and when he didn't answer I said, "over here on the floor." He took a step into the bothy. "I'm sorry," I said politely. Something moved at his feet and he stooped down to look. He shouted in Gaelic, and leapt back, threw his bundle into the corner and seized a piece of it.

With five or six horrible blows he beat about him downward, hitting by turns the boards and this soft thing. I heard scratching and shuffling and with the last blow a tearing moan that let loose in one hopeless breath more pain and horror, more unreasoning despair than my imagination could support. By the voice it was a woman, not a man. I flung myself past them and out through the door.

I climbed into the salmon boat to hide and I wept a lot there and tried to make up my mind what to do. But even here the fisherman did not let me be.

"Pass me yon rope there, ye," he said, looking over the side. "Man, man, there's no need to be afeared."

I saw then that it was Douglas Macrae, the West Highland man. I crawled out and gave him the rope.

"There's an awful mess made i' the bothy," he said, as we walked back toward it. "The lads told me for sure they had her killed and laid inside on the floor so there'd be nobody to interfere wi' her till Monday. And there's me coming home to my tea, and yourself and herself inside in it. Och man, there's eneuch o' greeting—wipe your eyes, that's a boy." He stood still and gave me a fishy brown handkerchief. "Anyways, she's dead—dead as a crow. But the Dear knows a selchie is hard killed. Yourself and me will drag her out and lay her by the midden."

"I didn't know it was a selchie," I said.

"There's only one way to kill a selchie and that's hit her to the nose. The back o' the head's no use—she's all fat there. The lads hit her on the head, I'm thinking, and had her stunned only. The life came back into her that way, as ye saw for yourself."

As we tied the rope round the dead body, I, standing in my bare feet on the bloody floor, tried to harden my heart to be like the old man. But it was action that stopped my tears. The body was thick and round, at least four feet long, and it took great strength to drag it out through the door across the pebbles to the midden. Its nose was battered, its eyes closed, its whole head clotted with blood, but its smooth belly shone sleek and even in the half light, a creamy fawn in color. Its back and flanks were mottled with dark spots, haphazard. When we took the rope off, it rolled over on its back and the two front flippers lay against its chest like hands—like human hands with five fingers webbed with skin. When the old man had his back turned, I felt the hands and stroked the long, round body.

He swilled the floor with buckets of water and swept it clean with a besom. He lit a fire with the dry wood he had gathered on the shore and we had mugs of tea and thick bread and butter by the light of a paraffin lamp. I noticed that he talked as quickly and as much with his mouth full as he did when it was empty, and I liked him better.

"Why did you kill the selchie?" I said.

"I wished it was not me that had the killing of her."

"Then why did you?"

"Did ye no' see her lying half alive there by the side o' the bed? It's me that's to sleep in the bed and if I put her out the door the way she was, alive, she would travel down to the sea again maybe and the lads would be at me o' Monday morning, thinking I sold her for the skin."

"You said it was unlucky to kill a seal."

"And so it is, the more if she's a selchie . . . "

"Then why . . . "

"The others had her killed afore me, did ye no' see that? It's a gey uncanny sicht to see a selchie on this coast. She was gone astray, I'm thinking. She's a stranger this side. She's come out o' the West some way. She's like myself." He looked across the table at me and stopped chewing. "It's no' an easy thing to live wi' strangers. Now if ye was at home in England, ye'd soon find yourself."

"I'm not English."

"Is that so? To hear ye speaking I thocht ye was. But wherever ye come from, it's no' the same away. No. No. In the West, now, folks are—well, a man's not so hard on himself for work nor money. If a man has his living fishing salmon he'll not be thinking of threepence here and sixpence there to be got from a day's work skinning a selchie."

"If he thinks it's unlucky he wouldn't. I expect he'd . . . "

"It's no' the skin that has the bad luck in it. The skin is lucky. Look here at this."

He handed me an old tobacco pouch made from a skin with short hair like the hair of the body by the midden.

"That pouch there has great luck in it. It is made of the paw of a

selchie, the right paw. I had that pouch there of my father and he
had it of his father and he made it. He was a seal-killer, my father's
father. I saw him once. He had a round cap, too, of the skin of a
selchie. I saw that cap. Would you like a jammy piece?"

"Yes, please."

"There was men that had their trade killing seals those days,
when folk did use to press the oil out o' the blubber and burn it in
lamps. There ye are now. Pass out the jam from the kist there, that's
the boy. And my grandfather was one. But I did hear my father say
he was oftentimes afraid because an awful thing did happen to one
that was before him in the trade—one by the name of Angus Ruadh
of Mallaig. Now the skin ye have in your hand there is never twice
the same. How would you say does it feel?"

"It feels nice. It's like . . . "

"Show me." He took it back and stroked it and began to fill his
pipe. "Aye. It's sleekit now. The hairs is lying even down like the
hairs of a sleepy cat. But in the morning likely they'll be standing
like the bristles of a sow. Did ye ever hear tell of another skin that
would live that way, after one hundred years?"

"What happened to Angus Ruadh?"

"That pouch there will change its color, too, following on the
tides."

"What happened to the man?"

"Och, there's no truth in it." He looked at me closely, shifting the
lamp. I saw the deep lines in his face and a kind look in his eyes. I
can now imagine what he saw in mine. "It's no use to frighten you,
and you to walk home the length of the carse in the darkness."

"I'm not frightened."

"Ye was frightened it's not long since."

"Anyway, I'll wait for the moon before I go."

"The moon will be up before midnight. All right so. 'What happened to him?' ye say. Well. Well, it happened one night when this
Angus Ruadh came home to his bothy, as it might be here, and laid
him down on the bunk, as it might be myself coming home with the

salmon, he was wakened by a stranger at the door, and this stranger says to him, darkening the door, 'Is your name Angus Ruadh, the seal-killer?' he says.

" 'That is my name,' says Angus. 'And what's your name?' he says. 'You look to be a stranger.'

" 'Never mind what's my name,' says this one. 'I am here to talk business,' says he, 'and I've no time to waste,' he says like an east-coast man.

" 'You're welcome anyways,' says Angus Ruadh, the seal-killer. 'Come in,' he says, 'and close the door and I'll wet the tea for you presently.'

" 'I thank you,' says the stranger, 'But I am pressed for time and the horse I have here does not like to stand. I'm come from a man that has money in his hand for you. Can you get him a hundred seal-skins?'

" 'A hundred sealskins!' says Angus Ruadh. 'That's a terrible number of sealskins,' says he.

" 'He'll take what you have in the house and give ye a year's contract after.'

" 'I'll best talk with him so,' says Angus Ruadh. 'Ye can bring me to your master at first light in the morning.' But the stranger says no, it must be this night. 'Ye can get up behind me on my horse,' he says, 'and I will bring ye to my master,' says he.

"Well, Angus Ruadh the seal-killer got up on the horse behind him and they took the road so fast that the wind that was in the back of them could not keep pace with them and the wind that was before them could not make away from them. And they came to a place where there was a great black cliff that overhung the sea four hundred feet below. And the horse stood by the cliffs edge and they got down off him, the stranger and Angus Ruadh.

" 'Are we gone astray?' says Angus Ruadh.

" 'No, Angus Ruadh,' says the stranger, and coming close before him he says, 'we are here.' Angus Ruadh, the seal-killer, made to look about him, but the stranger was always before him. 'And where is the person you spoke of?' says Angus Ruadh.

" 'You'll see,' says the stranger, and he came close and he took Angus in his two arms below the oxters with a strong grip and he pressed his body close to him and blew a long breath down into his mouth. And they were at the cliff's edge. And the stranger lifted Angus Ruadh and dived with him together down, down into the sea.

"They dived down into the darkness of the sea. They sank deep, and deep down on the sand and seaweed of the bottom they came to a door. Now the stranger opened this door and himself and Angus Ruadh walked in. And Angus Ruadh saw there a lot of rooms and a great multitude of folk that were greeting sorely and wailing. Says he to himself, 'I am here now for the rest of my days, for if I try to escape I'll be drowned surely.' And says he, 'If it's here I'm to live my days, with no green land or heather, and these folk wailing, it is not long my days will be.'

"Some o' the folks did feel for him, in spite of their own sadness, and three or four out o' them did try to give him comfort, but he could think of nothing but his own black thoughts. And suddenly the stranger was before him with a long sharp dirk in his hand. Angus Ruadh the seal-killer prayed mercy for his life.

" 'Did ye ever see this knife before?' says the stranger to him.

"He looked at it. 'I did,' says he. 'That's my knife,' says he, 'that you have there in your hand. It's my own knife that I lost this day hunting on the rocks.'

" 'Is that so?' says the man. 'Well, I mean you no harm.'

" 'I stuck that knife into a seal,' says Angus Ruadh, 'and the seal escaped with it into the water.'

" 'That seal was my father,' says the stranger.

" 'A seal your father?' says Angus Ruadh.

" 'He's lying here in the back room,' says the stranger. 'He's very sick and like to die,' says he, 'and it's only you can cure him. And I knew well,' he says, 'that there was no way to bring you to him only by a trick, and that,' says he, 'is all there is about the hundred seal-skins.'

"He showed him to his father within in the room and he was lying on the bed with a huge cut in his hindquarters. And there were more folk there about the bed and they told Angus Ruadh he must close the lips of the wound with his own hand; only his hands would do. And this he did. And immediately the wound was healed and the old seal rose up from his bed in perfect health. And there was great rejoicing round about.

" 'Now,' says the stranger to Angus Ruadh, the seal-killer, 'if you will make an oath before us now never to maim or kill another seal as long as you do live I will take you back to the land where you do live. For it is not good,' says he, 'to live among strangers.'

"Angus Ruadh swore a solemn oath and they went out the door. And the stranger took him again with his two arms below the oxters and gripped him the length of his body with a strong grip and they rose together up to the surface of the sea and when they stood together on the cliff's edge, four hundred feet above, the stranger blew a long breath down into his mouth. Well, the horse was standing there and the stranger put him up behind the saddle, and if they traveled fast when they came toward the cliff, they did travel twice as fast away from it, so fast that the wind that was in the back of them could not keep pace with them and the wind that was before them could not make away from them.

"So did this stranger put Angus Ruadh the seal-killer down at the cheek of his own door, and he made him a present which did keep him till he died without need to work. The present that the stranger made to Angus Ruadh the seal-killer was a bag of gold—Dane's gold. And that's what I have of the story."

The search party did not find me till the morning when I was on my way home, because I decided to sleep on the top bunk. I did not sleep much. I heard a horse and cart in the night and low voices talking and when I went out in the morning the selchie had gone from the midden. Neither the fisherman nor I spoke about it, but I knew he was snoring when the cart came and went, and I guessed by his silence that his turn had come to be afraid.

THE ANTITHESIS OF TIGH NA ROSAN WAS THE BLACK House, which I saw years later, a long, low building without windows or chimney, common in the Highlands and usual in the Hebrides up till about the year 1900. Douglas Macrae, the salmon fisherman, was born in a Black House, his father lived his whole life in one and his grandfather had probably never set foot in any other type of dwelling.

There are still many inhabited Black Houses in the northern parts of the Outer Hebrides, but the first I saw stood deserted near the shore on the island of South Uist. Werner Kissling showed it to me, in 1948, and I think he felt sad as we walked from the beach over the sandy grass, because it was there he had lived with a family of crofters when he first came to the island, and now, after burning for hundreds of years, their fire had gone out, they themselves were scattered, and their roof sagged low.

The house looked as though it was part of the ground. It was entrenched and lichened, like the boulders that sat nearby, its walls sloped inward toward the roof and its ends were rounded like the base of an old tower. The thatch where it was still undamaged was rounded too, and instead of forming eaves it rested on the middle of the wall. "The rain used to run through the center of the wall," said Werner. "But if you look at the way the stones are laid you can see how it never could run into the room." The walls were about three foot thick, built of rough granite without mortar, an outer and an inner course, with peat and rubble packed between them, and the stones of each course overlapped, sloping downward toward the outside to let the water drain through the loose center into the ground at the base. There are no trees on the island. The rafters were of driftwood and showed frayed marks made by sea and rocks. The door had probably been cut out of planks from some deck cargo, but it had long since been taken away to repair a neighbor's roof. We lowered our heads and went in. The broken thatch let in too much light.

"Even when the thatch looked perfect," said Werner, "your clothes would get splashed with tarry drops from above. The turf smoke made sticky black stuff up there somehow. I'm surprised the people have left so much of it here in the ruin, because it is valuable for manure. They would leave an old thatch on until it became thoroughly soaked in that peaty deposit from the smoke, then strip it and spread it on the land. In fact for that very reason they often left it too long for comfort and in bad weather we got dirty and wet."

He went on talking and looking above him, but by this time I had stopped listening because I saw we were not alone in the house. There were two children near us, a solemn boy, and a girl with long black hair, very slight, rare, elusive and beautiful. They were silent. We knew they had stood up silent when they heard us come near and now as each of us saw them we understood how we had rudely smashed the secret game they played in this old place.

Her right hand was clenched, the back of her left hand was against her mouth and her eyes stared fearfully at ours. She and her small brother backed away from us and stood against the wall steadily watching, hiding their mouths whenever we looked their way. I remarked on the slope of the floor, but according to Werner it had always been so. It was made of earth, beaten or trodden hard, and from the top of the room, on our right as we came in, where the family used to sleep, it fell away unevenly to the lower end where in the old days the cattle were stalled. In the middle of the floor there were a few blackened stones. Werner stooped down and sifted the old ashes with his fingers. "You've no idea," he said, "what a difference it made to a household to be able to sit round a fire—in a real circle, not a semi-circle like the ones we sit in now. That and the moving of the cattle out of the house. Those two were the first concrete signs of a change in the way we lived."

"We?"

"Except for the language I feel I could be one of this race. But the language is my great handicap still. You see I'm cut off from these children and shall remain so until they are old enough to learn English at school. I am cut off from their grandparents too—or most of them. Can you talk English, Mairi? Can you smoor the fire?"

"The fire is gone out."

"Oh you talk English well. Show me how you smoor the fire."

Mairi crouched still further into the wall.

"There was a prayer for that. There was a prayer for everything one did in the house and on the land. You raked the ashes over the red coals, to keep them in all night, and you made the Sign of the Cross over them and you said this prayer. I've forgotten the prayer. Mairi, do you remember the prayer?"

There was silence and we could hear the sea.

"Do you smoor the fire at home? Do you?"

"We have a black stove in our house."

"But you put the ashes over the cinders at night, don't you, to keep it alight till morning?"

"The black stove fire is quenched at night."

"And do you say a prayer over it?"

Silence.

"When I used to live in this house," said Werner, explaining his questions to them, "the woman of the house used to draw the Cross in the ashes with her finger and she said this prayer I am asking you about."

"I know how to smoor the fire."

"Do you?"

"My Aunt Kate Annie has one like that and it never goes out." She pointed to the ashes. "She asks for the Blessing at night."

"Is it in the middle of the room like this one?"

"It is not. She has a stone hearth and a grand chimney."

"Look, I'll pretend to smoor this one. I'll rake the ashes over and you say the prayer." Werner bent over the ashes again but she did not move from the wall. "Do tell me the prayer," he said.

"A person cannot smoor a fire that is dead."

"Are you Mairi Finlay?"

"I am."

"And is this your brother Angus?"

"It is."

"Are your grandfather and grandmother well?"

"They are." And in a whisper, "Thanks be to God."

"Will they be at home now if we go?"

Taking her brother by the hand she ran past us out of the door and stood a little way off, looking back as though she expected us to follow.

"It's as if she'd just seen how to escape from a trap," said Werner. "But I agree with her. I know she feels as I do. We are not like people talking to her. For her it must be as though some distant animal had suddenly come close and watched her, and then had tried to speak." We followed the children along the beach. The little girl came running back and held her clenched fist out to me.

I said, "What have you got there?"

She stood still and so did we. Then looking down at her hand she opened it slowly.

"It is a Mary bean," she said. "I am after finding it here on the shore."

"That's lucky," said Werner. "It has come a long way by sea."

She said, "It is very lucky, the Virgin Mary's bean."

"Where exactly did you find it?"

"Below the house beyond." She had a little brown nut, the size of an acorn but flatter.

"Will you give it to me for a moment?" She clutched it tightly and raced away to her brother ahead of us along the sand.

"What was it?" I asked Werner.

"A Molucca bean, whatever that is. They seem often to find them on the shore. I have two at home. They were given to me, but I've

been searching for years and never got one myself. They are supposed to come all the way to this coast by the Gulf Stream—from
South America or somewhere. They've been used as charms for
hundreds of years I know. Martin mentions them and that's two
hundred years ago. Charms against drowning—and against a whole
lot of evils."

I borrowed Martin's book from Werner later on and there I read
about the Virgin Mary bean. His *Description of the Western Islands
of Scotland* was published in 1703:

> There is variety of Nuts called *Molluka* Beans, some of which are
> used as Amulets against Witch-craft, or an Evil Eye, particularly
> the white one, and upon this account they are wore about Chil-
> dren's Necks, and if any Evil is intended to them, they say, the
> Nut changes into a black colour: That they did change colour, I
> found true by my own observation, but cannot be positive as to
> the Cause of it.
>
> MALCOLM CAMPBELL, Steward of *Harries,* told me that
> some weeks before my arrival there, all his Cows gave Blood
> instead of Milk for several days together, one of the Neighbours
> told his Wife that this must be Witch-craft, and it would be easy
> to remove it, if she would but take the White Nut, called *Virgin
> Maries* Nut, and lay it in the Pale into which she was to milk the
> Cows; this advice she presently followed, and having milked one
> Cow into the Pale with the Nut in it, the Milk was all Blood, and
> the Nut changed its colour into dark brown, she used the Nut
> again, and all the Cows gave pure good Milk, which they ascribe
> to the virtue of the Nut. This very nut *Mr Campbell* presented
> me with, and I keep it still by me.

We walked on without speaking. I was thinking of the Virgin
Mary bean and Werner had his eyes on the sand beneath our feet.
There were about twenty miles of sand ahead of us, fine and almost
white, a wide and gentle slope lined on one side by dunes clothed in
bent grass and on the other by long, even rollers curling white and
bottle green above the level of our heads.

Ronald Iain Finlay—or, to give him his full name, Ronald Iain, son of Ronald, son of Iain, son of Norman, son of Ronald—lived a few hundred yards above the shore, through the gap in the sand dunes where his granddaughter Mairi led us still holding her Mary bean in one hand and her brother by the other. We left the sandy grass, picked our way through outcrops of granite, piles of loose boulders and pools of peat water and came on to the rough track that led up to the house. I was disappointed when at last we caught sight of it to see that the Finlays' house was a modern Council house, square-built on one story out of concrete blocks and roofed with slate. The island people, as I discovered later, called it a White House and were naturally proud to possess one, but it seemed to us a strange economy that induced the County Council to ship cement and slates at huge freight charges from Glasgow to a country whose only real wealth exists in its own building material.

We went into a small room, the kitchen, and shook hands with Ronald Iain and his daughter, and after the teapot had stewed for fifteen minutes on the iron stove we had tea. Mairi whispered and buried her face deep into her mother's apron. Her mother laughed and smoothed her hair, and spoke in her own language.

"She says she's found a Mary bean," she said to us in English.

"Good girl. Good girl," said the old man. "Let me see. Oh it's a grand one, a big one isn't it?" He rolled it in his hand and sighed, picked it up and held it to the light, and then searched his pocket with stiff old fingers.

"It is larger than mine," he said, "and a lighter color. Look. It is the color of a good brown horse I would say."

He took a smaller bean from his pocket and laid them side by side. His was black and wrinkled, but where it was smooth it shone like polished ebony. "That Mary bean there was in my father's pocket on the day he died. I did take it from his inner pocket on the evening when his body came ashore."

"He was drowned," I said, stupidly, because I was surprised.

"He was, God have mercy on his soul: drowned sealing. There was three drowned with him and many drowned before him at the same trade."

"The charm was no good to him so," said Mairi's mother.

"Some has great faith in it at sea," he said to me, as though she had not spoken. "But I do think it only like a piece of stone or a bit of a strange-looking shell that some men will always carry with them. The boy there now—he found a stone with a hole in it and I have seen him crying if he's lost it, and if he should be put into the bed without it he'll never sleep, but as soon as you give it to him, into his hand, he will be quiet and sleep. It is a comfort to a person to have some little thing like that that's always with him. He'll turn it over in his hand, this way, and take comfort from it. I often heard my father say that if a man could have a piece of the skin of the King Otter, the size of a half a crown, he never would be drowned. But there's few has seen the King Otter, let alone killed him."

"Is it a special kind of otter?" said Werner.

"They say all the creatures of the water do have their own king. The King Otter does be pure white and as big as a lamb. I never saw him. I saw the King of the Seals myself though."

"What did he look like?" I said.

"Big. Big. An awful size of a seal. I never heard of a man killing him. No rope would hold him anyways."

The small boy, Angus, spoke at once in a high voice that stopped all thought of talk. He said, "A cotton rope would hold him."

There was a long minute's silence, and I knew he was ashamed. His grandfather took a sip of tea and stared at him. His mother blew her nose on her apron and stood still. I lit a cigarette and Werner looked at the pattern the tea leaves had made on the bottom of his cup.

The grandfather of Angus stared at Angus. Then he filled his pipe and lit it. Then he took it from his mouth. Then he said, "What kind of a rope do you say would hold the King Seal?"

"A cotton rope," said Angus, and this time he could hardly raise enough breath to pronounce the three words.

The old man puffed his pipe and looked at me. He said, "The boy there learns nothing at school. What is the strongest type of rope, boy?"

"I don't know," said the boy.

"You see, he learns nothing."

"They make rope out of hemp," said the boy. "And they make it at Dundee. But the best kind of rope for lungeing a young horse is cotton rope."

"Did they teach you that at school?"

"No. But I learned it off the factor when I went to tie the three-year-old to the gate post at the big house."

"He's always following the factor," said Ronald Iain. "He's always playing about by the big house. But at school he learns nothing."

"I tied him and he was frightened and he broke the rope I tied him with, and hurt his foreleg."

"Well."

"And the factor says if I tied him with white cotton rope he never would break loose."

"The factor is from Aberdeen," said Ronald Iain. "They do have all kinds of things on the mainland that we cannot get in the islands."

I said, "I think the factor is right."

"He is right for the mainland maybe, but the strongest rope on the islands is rope made out of horsehair. Your factor has rope, but he'll never know the strength of it till a boy like yourself ties a three-year-old and the three-year-old breaks away. But if I or my father used a rope of horsehair we would surely know the strength of it, and how to use it, because every inch of that rope would be made by ourselves. That is the difference between myself and the factor. That's where the old island ways is better. That's how you'll find you'll learn more with myself than ever you'll learn with school or the factor."

The boy went out of the house.

Werner said, "So it was horsehair rope they used for the seal net?"

"Amn't I telling you it was. The seal is the strongest swimmer in the sea. No other rope would hold her. But there's no rope at all would hold the King of the Seals and that's where the school and this factor from Aberdeen has the mind of the child destroyed."

"You spun the rope with your own hands?"

"We did, of course. We did not use the seal net in my day, but for every strong hold we used horsehair. We did make all kinds of things in the house at night as soon as darkness came, and you wouldn't remark the time passing in winter because the neighbors would be in and there would be music sung and stories told often far into the night, while we made harness and nets and the like. You never heard talk of the old seal net?" he said to me.

"No. I was told you used to kill the seals on land."

"That was the way in my father's day. But in his father's father's day, or maybe long years before that, they did use the seal net too. I don't know how long it would be since they laid it aside. But between two of the small islands near to North Uist there's a narrow channel and it was there in the old days that they used to catch the seals swimming, with this net."

"Like a salmon net?"

"It was made in the shape of a bag, but it was not altogether like the salmon net. The salmon net is made like the plan of the lobster pot. There's a neck leading into it, you understand, like a tundish or a funnel, and the salmon goes through to a wide bag beyond. But the neck of the seal net was made to draw close with the weight of the seal when she swam in. And if you have seen a seal in a salmon net and the raggedy holes she'll tear in it you'll know what power of rope was needed to hold her in a net of her own. My father was drowned by the weight of a seal."

"Tell me what happened," I said.

"I was with him in the boat at the time. And the seal that drowned him was the biggest I ever saw dead. By the mercy of God I was washed ashore safe, and I was fourteen years of age."

"The strength of the rope was no good to you that time," said the mother of the children, leaning over the stove with her back to us. I thought she said it in defense of her small son. The old man acknowledged her this time.

"It was the strength of the rope that swamped us. It was usual those times when we killed the seals ashore on the island to skin them where they lay and bring the skin and blubber home in the boat. But the island was only dry at low tide—it was what you might call a tidal rock—and if you delayed at your work too long you would be drowned and your boat lost. So now this day we were there—my father, myself and three of a crew—my father had a great bull seal killed and another near as big, and what way it was I forget, but he left the skinning of these two till the last, and when he came to them with his knife the other men stopped him and said it was time to make for home. The tide was well up and the sea was big and the wind was set for a storm. Well, of course, there was no way to make the dead seals fast that we might come at them again on the next ebb tide, and, they being such grand big ones, my father would not leave them to the sea. So we roped them well and took them in tow behind the boat. But the wind and tide was against us and out in the middle of the channel it was like as if we were rowing against a heavy stream.

"The sea came too high at the end. I remember how the weather was in my head and stomach and my hands were stiff and no right thought or word would come to me or any one of the men—only my father. He was laughing. And the last thing he said was that he thought it was the King Seal—the big one—by the weight of him. So the men made to row, but the weight of the bodies and the tide that pulled them took us sideways, sideways all the time against the oars. And the waves was rising that high with the white foam racing on the top o' them that our only hope was in taking them endways on, and this the power of four men could not do against the bodies of the seals. So we took water more and more. I had the tiller in the stern and I was watching the rope stretched tight and chafing and dragging this way and that against the boat. I could not see the seals. They was held there below in the water and they hung there deep, a deadweight with the tide against us. There was water to my knees in the boat and with one hand I was baling with a panny and with the other holding on to the tiller to try and hold the boat into the sea. When the big wave came on us the starboard side I was smothered and I thought I was on the floor of the boat. I was lying face down, but when I put out my hands there I could find no floor, nor no boat, but only the darkness of the water and it was deeper always. I was gasping a long while before I rose up. And I was choked for breath.

"Well, I was washed ashore beside the rocks half living, and it was my uncle that carried me home. And the cold was in me such as I think no man felt in him and lived after. But I lived. Give me another cup of tea, will you, Mary?"

As she poured the tea the mother of the children said, "I often wondered would I know what to do if they brought Angus home half drowned."

"Well, you'd do what came into your mind best to do."

"I suppose I'd put him by the fire with a blanket over him and I'd give him a drop of whisky, I suppose."

"It wasn't by the fire they put me," the old man said.

"It wasn't?"

"Although I do believe the fire would have roused me the same."

"Did they chafe your hands and give you whisky?"

"They did not. They put me down to lie between the two cows. There is no better warmth than the warmth of a cow."

Angus's mother clasped her hands and said, "Well, whoever would have thought of doing that?"

"It was a place we'd go and lie for ourselves oftentimes when we were children, if the night was cold."

"Dear me!"

"For you must remember the cows were with us in the house those times. It was only your mother, persuaded by the ways of the Sanitary Inspector and them that were willing to follow him, that first taught me to build a house for the animals outside, away from the fire. I never did think it was right to put them away from the fire. We did call the new animals' house a 'Ronald Laing House.' The name of this Sanitary Inspector was Ronald Laing, and it was he who first took a notion against having cattle in the house. But anyways they put me for warmth against the two cows that were lying close, and from there when I woke I could see the glimmer of the fire and my mother weeping by it, and twenty neighbors I suppose sitting round about. Did you ever see a Black House?" he asked me.

"I saw the ruins of one today."

"You'd get no comfort from a ruin. You'd have no thought, standing lonely in a ruin, of the warmth and the company that was in the old Black House. Had it any partitions, the one you saw?"

"I don't think so."

"Some people did build a partition between the sleeping room and the middle part where the fire was, and some again put a low wall between themselves and the place where the cattle were housed. And some again put in a small window of glass on the top of the wall. But my father and myself, we kept to the old way. We just had the one long room, and we had no window, only a hole by the eaves, a bit from the door, for to let the smoke away. So away above the fire, from where I was lying with the cows, I could see between the people to the box-beds and I could see my brother and sister looking out over the edge of the bed at me down the length of the room and they thinking, I daresay, that I might be dead. But I wasn't. I was feeling rightly now. But I lay there very still, watching, and they watching me. And when I did see them whisper together and look again at me, I did rise up my two hands and did shout. Oh, they climbed up over the side of the bed, like as if it was afire, and did run to my mother to hide in her skirts. I remember it well because I did laugh, and with laughing I coughed and felt bad again, and this disturbed the cows and they rose up on their knees and tumbled me to the floor. It was well after that to be brought to the fire and fed with milk, and all the folk about me praising God for my safety. My mother put her arm about me and everyone was quiet.

" 'Had you a seal roped to you?' she said. I told her Father thought it was the King Seal. 'But I think he was joking,' I said. 'He was laughing when he said it.'

"My uncle said, 'They were big ones so.' I told him they were big. 'They'll be washed ashore so. High tide is a half-hour after noon. They'll be washed ashore then. We'll go for them.'

"I said, 'I'll go with you.'

" 'I am sure you'll go with me,' he said, and I think everyone in the room was thinking of my father and the three of a crew that were with him and of when would they be washed ashore.

"I said, 'And the boat? What do you think Uncle Neil, what do you think would be left of the boat?'

"He said, 'I think there'll be a few spars in her . . . I think she'll be worth saving for to make the rafters of a house. Or maybe a table. You can make a right table from the spars of a boat.'

"My mother was weeping again, and I clung to the warmth of her, watching the faces about us. And the faces were steady. Well, there was an old man with his eyes on me and he had a big growth of hair on his head and face and his eyes were black and his name was Murtagh—Black Murtagh they did call him on account of his hair—and I remember he took the pipe from his mouth when all was quiet and did point the stem of it toward me. And he said, 'That boy was never reared for a seal-killer. This day is the last day of your house in the trade.'

"No one spoke. So I said, 'I am not afraid.' And Black Murtagh answered me: 'I know you're not afraid,' says he, 'but the luck of your house has turned and it's well for you to know it.'

" 'The luck of fishing turns,' said my Uncle Neil. 'And it comes back again. And on the land there's a bad harvest one year, and a poor winter after, but with the next harvest maybe a man's twice as well again.'

" 'The killing of seals is a thing of its own,' said Black Murtagh. 'The boy's father had word from his father against it, and this day's work has shown us.'

" 'Did you see something?' my mother said.

" 'I did,' said Black Murtagh. 'I saw it this day at noon.'

" 'While they were at sea,' said my mother, and she looked at him, holding me about the shoulders.

" 'Tell us what you saw,' said my uncle.

" 'I saw this boy on the shore,' said Black Murtagh, 'and he with five coffins by him trying with all his strength to draw them back one by one through the sand so the waves of the sea couldn't touch them.'

" 'There was five in the boat,' said my mother, whispering.

" 'And I saw two seals come ashore to him, swept in by the same waves. And the two seals did take off their skins and, when they did, two young women stood by this boy. And they went one either side of him. And they made to shift a coffin each. But the strength of the sea carried those coffins from them. So they went to another two coffins and this boy was between them looking on to the coffin in the center. And the two seal women tried to draw these coffins back away from the waves. But it was no use again, for didn't an awful size of a wave come and swamped them and left them there on the shore again with the second two coffins swept away out of their hands. And I couldn't see the boy. But when the wave drew back I saw the boy standing there half drowned, and he holding on to this last of the coffins with every bit of strength he had left in him.'

" 'Well!' said my mother. And Black Murtagh rose to his feet, and put his hand over his head so high we couldn't see it for the smoke above in the rafters. And to look at him put the heart across me, belted around with the smoke as he was, the upper half of him above us—we in awful circle round the fire. And he stooped down again and pointed to me with the stem of his pipe.

" 'Didn't the two seal women come to this boy,' said Black Murtagh. 'And didn't they together with him draw his own coffin back away from the sea and lay it high on a bank of grass above.'

"There was silence again in the room. 'Was there any other thing you saw?' said Neil, my uncle.

" 'There was one other thing,' said Black Murtagh. 'And that was the last of it. I saw the two seal women sit down on the coffin and they weeping by it. And I saw this boy go down on the shore and gather up the two sealskins and bring the two to them. And the two seal women stopped weeping then, and they took the skins from the boy and went back into the sea.' "

As he told this story, Ronald Iain had become more and more excited, acting each part with his hands and head until at the end, when he came to the point where Black Murtagh stood up, he stood himself with a hand above his head and declaimed the last part of Murtagh's vision. He sat down now and spoke in his ordinary voice. "I never did go sealing any more," he said. "I went out at noon with my uncle and a crowd of men and the first thing we did drag ashore was the body of my father, and the second then was the bodies of the seals, tied together with the rope. The boat was smashed, but the rope itself was good. It was attached yet to one of the seats of the boat where we tied it, but the seat itself had come adrift on the rocks. Well, the bodies of the men were washed ashore through the next two days in several parts of the island."

"Did anyone take over the seal hunting after you?" I asked him.

"No. No. There might be an odd party go out once a year to the seal place where they came ashore to breed. They used to beat them with clubs there on the shore to kill them. But when I was a boy there was beginning to be less and less call for seals and it soon came so as no one would be able to make a living out o' them."

" 'Twas the paraffin oil killed that trade," said Angus's mother.

"That, and the rubber seaboots. The old people did use the skins for all kinds of things. One time long ago they did cut it in strips and use it like straps, or say for the traces of a horse's harness. They'd make seaboots of it too, and purses and caps and the like. They'd eat the flesh too in my father's day. There was a terrible smell off the flesh. But we never had use for that. When we had the skin stripped from the body we'd take the blubber off. This was the main use of the seal. And we'd press the blubber on boards beneath big stones and draw the oil out for lighting. That was the only light we had at that time. We did use to put the oil into a crusie lamp with a wick of rushes floating in it. Folk would laugh now at the small glimmer of light we were content with. Mairi, will you show them the grand new lamp we have. 'Tis dark enough now for to light it."

"I'll bring it," said Angus. "I'll light it." No one had noticed him come back into the room. And now he slipped out in bare feet and came back slowly, holding a pressure lamp in both hands like a priest with a chalice.

"My sister sent it from Glasgow," his grandfather said. "I don't know if ever you saw one as good. Where does the oil come from, Angus? Did they teach you that at school?"

"It comes on the ship from Mallaig."

"It does. And before that, where does it come from?"

"It comes from Glasgow."

"And before that?"

"It comes in another ship before that."

"It does. It comes from Mexico they say."

"My Mary bean comes from Mexico," said Mairi.

"Who told you that?"

"The man says it comes a long way by the sea."

"Let me look at it again, will you, child?" She brought it over to him and he laid his own beside it under the glaring light of the lamp.

"It's wonderful the difference in the color," he said. "You can remark it more clearly by this light. Now this bean here was black as you see it now when I took it off my father after he being drowned. But my mother when she saw it did declare it was light and brown on the morning before we went out after the seals."

Mairi leaned on the table, her head sideways with her cheek against her arms, her black hair falling down across the Virgin Mary beans, and I noticed for the first time that one of her eyes was blue and the other brown. Her skin was fair. The old man moved her hair gently and put the brown Mary bean into her hand.

"Will mine go black?" she said. "I think I'd like it to be black like yours."

"Don't say that, child. With the help of God, yours never will turn black."

We prepared to leave, but Mairi's mother was breaking pieces of peat and putting them into the stove.

"You'll have another cup of tea before you go," she said. "And I am sorry to delay you, but these sods of peat are cut too big for the stove."

"Did you see many stoves like that on the mainland?" the old man said to me.

"Yes. But I think they are really made for coal."

"They're grand and warm, but I wonder couldn't they build them so that a person might watch the red of the fire."

"The hole at the top is too small for peat," I said.

"Well, I do think the peats burn better on the ground or on a flat hearth, and there's no trouble then with the size of them. This woman spends half her day breaking peats."

- "If they're the hard black peats, I cannot break them," she said.

"Wouldn't you rather have the old type of fireplace?" said Werner.

"Well now, I don't know. It is this kind they have in all the White Houses."

"They go out at night Mairi tells me."

"Did she tell you that? Well, it's hard to keep them in, that's true. But we try. Is that what you told the man, Mairi?"

She answered her mother in Gaelic, and her mother laughed.

"Well you know the prayer, don't you? You could have told the man the prayer. She will say it for you now," she said to us. But Mairi ran out of the room.

"Will you say it?"

"I'll say the one my mother used."

She sat down on a chair and spoke in a monotone the words of a Gaelic rhyme. I was not able to understand it or to write it down, but as I learned later there are many prayers used for smooring the fire. In *Carmina Gadelica* (Edinburgh, 1900) Alexander Carmichael published several of the Scottish versions with his own translation. Of these I have chosen one that seems in rhythm near to what Mairi's mother spoke that night.

> The sacred Three
> To save,
> To shield,
> To surround
> The hearth,
> The house,

The household
This eve,
This night,
Oh! this eve,
This night,
And every night,
Each single night.
Amen.

In Ireland, too, I was shown how to smoor a peat fire at night, or "rake the fire" as they call it there, but until I read Carmichael's note on the subject I thought only of its practical purpose. Carmichael says:

The ceremony of smooring the fire is artistic and symbolic, and is performed with loving care. The embers are evenly spread on the hearth which is generally in the middle of the floor—and formed into a circle. This circle is then divided into three equal sections, a small boss being left in the middle. A peat is laid between each section, each peat touching the boss, which forms a common centre. The first peat is laid down in name of the God of Life, the second in name of the God of Peace, the third in name of the God of Grace. The centre is then covered over with ashes sufficient to subdue but not to extinguish the fire in name of the Three of Light. The heap slightly raised in the centre is called 'Tulla nan Tri', the Hearth of the Three. When the smooring operation is complete the woman closes her eyes, stretches her hand, and softly intones one of the many formulae current for these occasions.

AFTER MY FIRST VISIT TO THE HEBRIDES, I WENT TO Ireland and there met Séamus Delargy, who had promised to help me in my pursuit of seals. He took me to County Kerry. The first part of the journey was somber, especially for him, because he drove by way of Cork to attend the funeral of the Irish scholar Dr. Osborn Bergin, whose friend and disciple he had been for thirty years. It was Bergin who had advised Delargy while he was a student to perfect his study of the Irish language by learning the Munster form of speech. So he went to a village near Bolus Head in County Kerry and there in the house of a great storyteller—Seán Ó Conaill—he started as a language exercise to note down traditional stories word for word. He soon became interested in the stories for their own sake, and so began almost by chance the huge collection of music and oral tradition now so well organized under his leadership by the Irish Folklore Commission. It was not difficult, I found, to make him share my mania for seals.

The city of Cork that day was cold and dismal, not as I have known it when its ships and mad street traffic make one feel alive and searching. When we left, we took the road to the west, but at first, with suburban houses and petrol stations in the drizzle, it seemed like any bleak way out of any city. We drove through Macroom, Ballyvourney and Killarney, over the mountains and steeply down to Waterville on the Atlantic shore.

In places we could see the old Butter Track winding up and down the mountains by our road. Cork used to be the main butter market for the whole of Munster. Old tracks led to it from every side, and along them through the years before carts became common and railways were built the butter carriers made long journeys on foot in bands of twenty men or more, against the robbers, leading strings of pack horses laden with firkins of butter to be sold. Séamus Delargy spoke about them as we drove along their route. Their journey from Southwest Kerry, to which we were bound, took several days. They had regular stopping places, like Ballyvourney or Macroom, and a great part of their day and of their evening's rest was spent in telling stories.

A red stag got up and crossed in front of us a few miles on from Killarney. It loped across the road as though it was accustomed to cars. There were no people. The ground near the top of the pass where we stopped to look back over the Lakes of Killarney was sodden and green and brown, smelling to me of the days of my boyhood when we slept in a tent in the Highlands of Scotland and ate raw eggs and midges whipped up together in a bowl. Further on we came in to an open valley with green fields, stone walls and brown, uneven hills on either side. These things and the thoughts of childhood I consciously liked, but the sudden blue flash of the sea as we turned a bend in the hills above Kenmare Bay was a shock which brought us both out of the gray mood that had sat on us in Cork, in spite of the quays and whisky, in spite of the ships from Stavanger and Cardiff and the Clyde. We were still in shadow, but the sun was on the sea. And again, still more brightly and as sudden, we saw the sunset over Ballinskelligs Bay.

Three little islands stand high in the water far out beyond the bay. They changed their shape and color every hour or so while we were there, lying sometimes in the sky, sometimes low and flattish, often pointing high like cones. They used to be inhabited by the souls of the dead. They were called in old Irish "Tech Duinn"—the House of Duinn, god of Death—and they held all the dead of Ireland. Waterville lies north of them, roughly in the middle of the curve of the bay, and unlike Reen Eeragh and Bolus Head it has a gentle shore. In Waterville we went to see Tadhg Tracy.

Tadhg Tracy is the schoolmaster, and like so many country schoolmasters in Ireland he is gifted, humane and inspiring to others. He speaks Irish and English with equal ease and everything I learned in his part of the country I learned with his help as guide and interpreter.

He told me by the lakeside, while the fine rain blew into our backs, of the "hedge schools" where his father was educated under English rule. Here, where the English language still had to be painfully acquired, any boy heard speaking a word of Irish in school would have the "Cingulum" put on him. It was a thick, straw collar. He would have to wear it round his neck until he caught another boy speaking Irish. That gave him the right to transfer it; an aspect of the team spirit less humiliating perhaps than it sounds, for it may have seemed at the time like a game and no child would know how destructive it was in intention and effect. The men who administered the rule were, of course, Irish, but their books and methods came to them from the ruling nation under a system similar to that which was instituted in India during the nineteenth century, and their pupils, odd though it now seems, having grown up bi-lingual, used to beat their own children if they heard them speak a word of Irish at home, for no one could get a good job unless he knew English. And now, too late by one generation, Irish parents and government are trying to put their own language back into the mouths and minds of the grandchildren of those hedge-school boys. It is impossible now to get a good job unless you know Irish: post office, customs, police, and, of course, the teaching profession, all demand it. I know one small boy who is not allowed any sugar if he speaks a word of English at meals.

Tadhg's father attended the hedge school at Castlecove. It was held there, as in other places, between the months of May and August, usually in the cowsheds when the cows were out on grass. The schoolmasters, Tadhg told me, were often known as "poor scholars," because many of them were men who had been to college for some time in preparation for the priesthood but had been for various reasons unable to remain there. They had a smattering of classical knowledge and were looked on as learned men. Some of them were learned, but many were men who had no other chance of earning their living—cripples or invalids—and some were even soft in the head. They fed and lodged one night at the house of each boy in turn.

"The boys made their own ink from acorns," Tadhg said. "There were no seats in the school, only stones, and one of these masters that taught my father, he used to greet the boys in the morning with a shout: 'Out for moss, boys!'—for he intended every day to put cushions on the stones. So they would all run out up the hill and stay the whole day long, and when they came back in the evenings he would try to punish them, but he could never reach them because he had only one leg. There was another whose principal faith was in noise. That's to say he believed that noise was a sign of activity in school and that activity itself was the mark of learning. So he would put a boy on the roadside as a lookout and if the landlord or the priest came by he'd get warning. 'Make noise!' he'd shout then, 'Make noise will you!' And the school would keep shouting and gabbling until the danger was past."

But in spite of such eccentricities, the children learned to read. Their first book was always *The Universal Spelling Book*. It consisted of pages called Meaning Slips, of which Tadhg remembers a few. The first was "A-b-l-e—Abel—A Man's name; able to work, able to do"; and the last was "Zodiac—a track of the sun showing the three great signs of three great circles." They learned the Meaning Slips at home, and in the cowshed next day they chanted them out like a prayer, but a difficult word like "rhinoceros" would usually be passed over. "Reen-o-*sair*-us," one boy said, unable to pronounce it. "How do you say it?" he asked. "Oh that is a beast of the negro kind. Skip that, boy. A dirty old beast."

But if the master knew the word and the boy didn't, the boy was whipped on the legs.

"There was one master," Tadhg said, "and he had a very bad temper. And there was a boy who had not learnt his Meaning Slip. So this boy was standing before the master, shaking with fear on one leg for fear of the whip. But before he could start to show his ignorance in came one of the parents—another hot man—and started an argument with the master, the two of them standing up by this boy. 'I say it is!' said the master. 'I say it isn't!' said the other, and this continued like an angry chant for some time. So while their minds were occupied the boy began to chant too, as though from his Meaning Slip: 'I say it is, I say it isn't,' over and over again, until when the argument was over the master believed that his task was done."

The next book was *Reading Made Easy.* Tadhg remembered Lesson 1—a picture of a Chinese man and a tea bush, with these words underneath it: "This man came from China to sell his tea. It grows on small trees in his country and is very nice for a boy's breakfast."

But tea was unknown in the countryside of Ireland when Tadhg's father was a boy. The only people who had tasted it would be those who had made the journey to Cork, where, as a treat, they drank great quantities of it out of quart "cuckie bowls" until they were sick.

Later on Tadhg's father studied the *Principles of Politeness,* a selection of Chesterfield's letters to his son—"directing the young man's steps and teaching him how to make his way among the crowd." Tadhg had with great enjoyment committed to memory the fragments he had heard his father recite.

An awkward country fellow, when he comes into company better than himself, is exceedingly disconcerted. He knows not what to do with his hands or his hat, but either puts one of them in his pocket and dangles the other by his side; or perhaps twirls his hat on his fingers, or fumbles with the button. If spoken to he is in a much worse situation, he answers with the utmost difficulty and nearly stammers; whereas a gentleman, who is acquainted with life, enters a room with gracefulness and a modest assurance, addresses even persons he does not know, in an easy and natural manner, and without the least embarrassment . . .

One may always know a gentleman by the state of his hands and nails . . . When the nails are cut down to the quick it is a shrewd sign that the man is a mechanic, to whom long nails would be troublesome, or that he gets his bread by fiddling; and if they are longer than his finger ends, and encircled with a black rim, it foretells he has been laboriously and meanly employed, and too fatigued to clean himself: a good apology for want of cleanliness in a mechanic but the greatest disgrace that can attend a gentleman . . .

Pulling out your watch in company unasked either at home or abroad, is a mark of ill-breeding . . .

Eating quick, or very slow, at meals is characteristic of the vulgar; the first infers poverty, that you have not had a good meal for some time; the last, if abroad, that you dislike your entertainment . . .

Spitting on the carpet is a nasty practice, and shocking in a man of liberal education. Was this to become general, it would be as necessary to change the carpets as the table-cloths; besides it will lead our acquaintance to suppose that we have not been used to genteel furniture; for this reason alone, if for no other, by all means, avoid it . . .

With these principles in mind, the boys went home to houses like the one Tadhg brought me to next evening.

We climbed the southern arm of Ballinskelligs Bay up a steep road with one green field between us and the rising cliff, a black mountain ahead, shaped like the sugar loaves old people speak of, the sun behind it most of the time and red in our eyes as the road turned. To our right across the sea was Bolus Head, behind us the mountains. The seal-killer's house was high in the hillside, two miles from any other. By the time we reached it daylight had gone, and everything smelt of rain.

The seal-killer's name is Sean Sweeney. He was eighty that year, a small man with a long back and short legs that had once been famous for their quickness. He had left the top half of his door open and we saw his silhouette against the light inside, where he rested on his elbows trying to see who was coming. Tadhg shouted. Sean shouted, pulled back the bottom of the door and came stiffly down the hill to meet us, talking all the way in high tones which did not get any quieter as we met. Then we climbed up the path to his house.

His house had one room only, dim, shadowy and warm, a wide hearth to the right as we came in, with a turf fire burning in its center, a fringe of curtain hanging over the mantelpiece, a large hunk of bacon above it on a nail and a set of black leather harness on a peg at one side. There was what they call a "rack" against the far wall— a wide bench, wooden, with back and arms. Séamus and I sat on that. And beneath the window, against the front wall, there was an ordinary kitchen table covered with oilcloth, with two wooden chairs beside it. Sean Sweeney and Tadhg sat on these. Sean, at least, had never spent an evening on a softer seat. A paraffin lamp hung above his head, and above ours a little red one shining upward on a picture of the Sacred Heart. In a corner by the door some steep wooden stairs led up to the loft, which stretched half-way over the room and seemed when you stood under it like a piece of a wooden ceiling that the builder had left unfinished. In fact it was used as an upper story. The children of the house had slept there once, and Sean, after long years of looking after them, for his parents had died young of a fever, now slept up there by himself. He had never married, he told us, because there were so many younger than he that needed caring for. The loft had a low wooden parapet. It was like a small balcony overlooking the hearth.

Sean was a fast and lively talker. His hands were huge and never still. He used them together as he spoke, as though pushing the words toward you, or sometimes to shade his eyes or his mouth from you in shyness. He spoke no English, and Tadhg, who was acting as interpreter for me, had brutally to break a flow of local genealogies and names. "Your father was a seal-killer," said Tadhg, knowing the way I wanted the talk to turn.

"He was," said Sean, "and I went after them too."

"Well, tell us about that if you can."

"There's little to tell in my day. Because in my young day there was little chance of killing seals, and that was on account of the land-lord we had here in those times. That landlord, he knew those seals as you or I would know our own cows, each one."

I said, "Does he mean he thought he owned the seals? Had he some sort of right to them or what?" I expected Tadhg to interpret, but he said something else to Sean and I had to interrupt to find out what it was. In fact I had to interrupt so often that I shall not put down the halting zigzags of our conversation here.

Tadhg said, "Do you remember the tailor in the loft?" Sean did not remember. Tadhg said, "It was a loft the same as yours there, with the little wooden paling, and if you stood in it you would look down on the hearth and see the people sitting round the fire, enjoy-ing themselves in conversation, but if you were to crouch down, or lie down for yourself up there, you'd hear everything that passed below and no one was to know a person would be up there. That's what the tailor was at when he lay in the loft."

"Is that so?" said Sean, or at least he showed some such sign of tactful interest.

Tadhg said, "My father often told me of the tailor," and Sean cut off a slice of plug, rubbed it in his hands and took his pipe from his pocket.

"Now this tailor," said Tadhg. "You remember the old traveling tailors better than I do."

"I do," said Sean, and took a red piece of turf from the fire with the tongs to light his pipe. "I remember them well," he said after he had lit it. And for some reason we all remained silent until the pipe was lit. "This suit of mine was made by one of those tailors," said Sean, "and there's wear in it yet. That's the kind of tailors we had those times."

"They went from house to house making clothes for the people," said Tadhg, "and whatever house they went to, there they would stay until the work for that house was finished, and they'd get their bit to eat and a place to lie down for themselves every night, for what time they stayed in that house."

"They would, they would. That's true," said Sean, puffing.

"And a great number of tailors were great storytellers," said Tadhg. "I remember 'twas a thing we'd all look forward to, the visit of the tailor, because of the long stories he'd tell by the fire at night. 'Twas a thing you'd expect of a tailor, to be able to tell stories, for when he was able to make clothes and travel, he was surely well able for that."

"If he wasn't able for stories," said Sean, "the people those times would hardly think him fit to remain in the house making clothes."

"Well, this tailor of the loft was that kind," said Tadhg. "And for years he'd been coming to this house near to my father's house, not more than three miles from where we are now. And the man of this house was a great storyteller himself. Oh, the people came far to his house to hear stories and they'd sit all night listening to him there. And this tailor that used to be traveling the roads, he himself was a storyteller nearly as good and he knew the most of the old man's stories himself, only for one great story that he never could get off him. And the name of that one was 'King Cormac and King Conn.'"

"I heard it," said Sean.

"Well, the tailor never could get to hear it."

"Why so?"

"Because the man of the house didn't want him to hear it. He was kind of jealous of it, or something, and he never would tell this particular story when he knew the tailor was there. But other nights he would tell it, and the people expected him to tell it; it was the best of all his stories, and he knew that and all the people knew that. And it took more than an hour in the telling. But this tailor of the loft, though he tried the old man with pleading and praying, and tried him with flattery and tried him with envy by saying his own were the better stories, he never could get to hear it. Well, it was two years since the day they saw the tailor in that house, and a year since they saw him in this district itself, and the man of the house was settled down by the corner of the fire, and a grand moonlight night it was that brought people from far to his house, and his house was crowded full of people, some sitting on the table and benches and some standing, and many young ones and children on the floor. And the old man commenced the evening with a story. And what story was it but 'The Story of King Cormac and King Conn.' And they sat listening. And he told it, and if he told it that night he told it well. He told it better, I heard my father say, than ever he had told it before. And the people were quiet through it for more than an hour. You've seen them so, Sean, in the old days—a whole house of twenty or fifty people in a room like this room here, and they listening quiet except for a word here and there to encourage the storyteller or to remark on the wonder of it, now at this place, now at that. And at the latter end when he was at the finish the whole house was in a hush. Not one of these persons did move from where they were. But up jumps your man, then, the tailor! Above in the loft a small little man, and his head and shoulders at the wooden paling above, as it might be there, Sean, looking down on your hearth. 'I have it,' he shouts, and his voice is high, like a little pipe. 'I have it now!' and he's down the ladder with that and out the door."

"He'd been in hide, up there," said Sean, "the whole night. Man, man, but wasn't he the right one for it!"

"He was. And he had the right memory too, Sean. From that night, he had the story, as good in every word as the words of the man of the house. And he told it after that wherever he went tailoring until the day he died. But he never dared go more to that house, that was all."

"Man, man, that's good," said Sean, and laughed. "Have you that story, Tadhg?"

"I do know it, but I haven't it complete."

" 'Tis about the King Otter."

"That's the one," Tadhg said.

"And how with the enchantment that was on him the king was never able to sleep."

"You have it yourself?"

"I have," said Sean. "And I remember how they used to say that anyone that's born of the water is not able to sleep. 'Tis like as if the movement of the water was always with them in their head."

"Well, I suppose," said Tadhg, "we never heard of a fish sleeping."

"No. But I don't know."

" 'Tis hard to imagine a fish sleeping," said Tadhg. "But I do believe by what I remember of the nature books that it says there they do sleep. And the otter, well now, the otter he does make a place for himself under the bank of the river, and I do believe he'll go to sleep in there."

"If he does," said Sean, " 'tis with one eye open."

"Maybe."

"And the seal."

"Well, we've all seen the seal asleep surely. And in the daytime itself, lying there on the strand in the sun."

"But did you ever go to shoot him," said Sean, "and you thinking him asleep?"

"I never shot a seal," Tadhg said.

"He'll see you and he'll smell you, and he, as you'd think, dead asleep, and he'll make for the water. 'Tis only on account of him being slow and clumsy on the land that you'll come at him. 'Twas the same thing in the seal caves when the hunt was on. No, Tadhg, if he sleeps at all it is with one eye open, himself and the otter the same. Now look at the cat there," said Sean, holding his big hands out toward her as she lay in front of the fire. "She is sleeping there like a Christian, the same as an old dog. When he sleeps, he sleeps. And he'll dream, itself. I often heard my old dog dreaming he was after a hare on the hill, calling out in his sleep, kind of muffled in his voice, and his legs and tail moving, but only half moving. But in his head there the hunt was on. And I know surely he sleeps like a Christian. I've seen an old mare, and she asleep every night standing up on her four feet, and her head nodding in her sleep and her eyes shut—sound, sound asleep the way you could stand close by her, if you went quietly, and she not know it. I know the fox does sleep too. He is wary too, more so than the otter and the seal, but he'll sleep for himself in his den the most part of the day like a dog. And with any kind of fowl, can't you go to them in the night and lift the wildest of them down from her perch, and she asleep. But in the daytime you couldn't come near her. With the hare and the rabbit and the rat and the mouse and all the creatures of the land you'll find they do waken and go asleep the same as we do. But for them that has the tides of the sea running through them from the day they are born until the day they die there is no such a thing as sleep the way we know it."

"And if that is true," said Tadhg, "it is a terrible torment to think of."

"When my mother died of the fever," said Sean, "and I a young lad at the time, the power of sleep was away from me for seven full nights and days."

I asked Sean Sweeney to tell us the story of King Cormac and King Conn, and after a silence he began.

"When Cormac was King of Ireland he had palaces in many places," said Sean, "and when summer came around he used to go to them to stay for a while amusing himself and finding out how the country was getting on.

"He had one son, and he died. But his three daughters were as fine as an eye ever saw. Nothing troubled them morning or night but sport and pleasure—walking on the shore, swimming and such amusements. And when King Cormac returned home each evening they met him with laughter and kisses.

"Things went on like that until a very warm summer came, and Cormac decided on the first of June to travel all round Ireland with his queen, who was old, to spend a while in each of the palaces. You often heard that when the cat leaves home the mice can dance, and that was the way with Cormac's daughters!

"There was a big lake below the palace, and nothing would do them but go swimming there, though they had orders not to do so. One very warm day the three went out swimming: the youngest wasn't as sturdy as the other two. When they were in the middle of the lake a big animal came to the surface near them, and what was he but an otter! The three made for the shore as fast as they could, and the otter after them. He caught up with the young one and lay beside her as she swam till they were near the shore. The two eldest ran away screaming to the servants that their sister was killed by the otter, and when the servants rushed down to the edge of the lake they met the young one walking toward the palace, and nothing wrong with her at all. They were delighted to see that she was alive. But wait until you hear the rest of the story—'tis as true as a prayer!

"The time passed by and Cormac sent a message home that he would return on such a day. The neighbors and servants and, of course, the daughters were overjoyed. The three went a few miles along the road to meet the King, and when they saw him coming toward them they ran to shake his hand and to kiss him. The two eldest were ahead and the young daughter last. She stretched out her hand to welcome her father.

" 'Clear out of my sight,' shouted the King. 'When I left home three months ago you had the look of a maiden in your eye and the bloom of youth in your cheek, but today you look to be carrying a child.'

"Off the creature ran, crying. Cormac entered the palace, made off to the big room and sat on his fine throne. The servants were in and out getting ready a meal. He sent for the youngest daughter that he wanted to talk to her. 'What do you want me for, Father?' says she. 'Go down on your two knees there on the floor,' says the king, 'and tell me what happened to you since I went away, or I'll put my sword through you.'

"At long last she told him, and she crying and bawling, about the otter and what happened to her in the lake.

" 'I believe what you say,' says the King. 'And if you told me anything but the truth, I'd cut off your head. I understand that you couldn't help what happened, and who knows but 'tis all for the best.'

"Very well, the time passed, and they had to look around for a midwife for the young daughter. She gave birth to a fine son without any trouble, and when the King heard the news he was delighted, as his own son had died. There's no telling about the care that was taken of the child—they carried him out of the house on their shoulders and back the same way. He had to be given everything he asked for. And he grew big like a young goose!

"When he was seven years old he was sent to school and he learned all he was taught. After that he used to go everywhere with King Cormac, and he always called the King 'father'—the child didn't know the truth! One day as they were walking along the edge of the strand Cormac complained that he was feeling tired.

" 'I have been watching you for the last couple of years, Father,' says the young lad, 'and I notice that you are losing ground and getting stiff with old age. You'd better give the crown and the ruling of the kingdom over to me. I'm fine and young and clever enough to look after your affairs and you won't have to stir outside the palace any longer.'

" 'What's putting that idea into your head, my child?' says Cormac. 'Soon enough you'll have the ruling of this kingdom! Who else is there for it?'

"A good while after that, they were out together another day and the old king again complained of being tired.

" 'You'd better hand over the rule of the kingdom to me,' says the lad again, 'and you can remain at home.'

"Things were left like that for a long while, and the young lad said the same thing another day.

" 'Whoever puts notions like that into your childish head, he's no friend of yours,' says the King. 'I don't feel like handing up the crown to you as long as I can move about myself. You'll get it in good time, as I have no son of my own.'

"At that the young lad spoke with anger: 'If you don't give it up to me of your own free will,' says he, 'I will make you give it to me!'

"On reaching the palace, the young fellow asked his mother to get food for a journey ready for him.

" 'What's the matter with you, dear?' says the mother.

" 'My father won't give me the crown or let me rule,' says the son. 'And as he won't give it to me freely, I'll take it from him by force.'

"The mother didn't take much notice of that, but then he got sulky toward them all and they couldn't satisfy him. He took the food along with him and traveled on till evening and the end of the day came. He saw a light in a house by the roadside, and in with him. The old hag that was living there knew him well—wasn't he the King's son? He got a great welcome and asked if he could stay till morning. Next morning he asked her did she know any place where he might get work, or where did Fionn Mac Cúil live. She told as well as she could how far away Fionn's court was.

" 'You'll get plenty work there,' says she, 'you should be there around nightfall when the soldiers are coming home.'

"Very well, he set off again, and reached Fionn's court and dwelling at nightfall, just as the soldiers were returning. He asked them where their master was. Then Fionn appeared and he asked him for a job.

" 'What pay would you be looking for?' says Fionn.

" 'Let this be the bargain,' says the young fellow. 'I'll stay with you for a year and a day, and if you have any fault to find with me, pay me what you like. If you don't find any fault with me you must pay me what I ask.'

" ' 'Tis a fair bargain,' says Fionn.

"Fionn thought there wasn't anybody that he couldn't find some fault with. And so the young fellow started his service with Fionn.

"Poor King Cormac was at home in his palace, full of age and worry. Near his palace was a small house where a smith called Gaibhne Gow lived; he kept shoes under Cormac's horses and looked after them and kept an eye on things around the palace. He had three daughters and the youngest of them was sixteen or seventeen years of age. King Cormac went to the smith and told him to send his youngest daughter as a servant to the palace.

" 'She'll be well looked after there,' says the King. 'And 'twill be to your own benefit.'

"The smith promised gladly to send her and she went to the palace. She wasn't two days there when the old queen died of a broken heart on account of her grandson having left the palace. King Cormac was more lonely than ever when the queen died and the young lad had left, and he prayed every day that God would prosper him. Then one day he got notion of marrying the smith's daughter— God might send him an heir to take up the throne after him. He spoke to the girl; she was still very young, but in any case she agreed to marry the King. They got married in the way that was customary at the time.

"Things went on till the year and day were nearly up by the young fellow in the service of Fionn. The thought struck Fionn that if he didn't find some fault with the lad he might take all his power from him. So Fionn went off to an old blind man who had the gift of knowledge and told him how things were.

" 'If I can find fault with him, I can pay him what I like,' says Fionn.

" 'That's quickly done,' says the old man. 'Leave your sword outside the door tonight and remain awake yourself. When it is around two or three o'clock call the lad by name to bring it in, and if he doesn't answer you have fault to find with him!'

" 'I'll try it,' says Fionn.

"Fionn went home and when they had all gone to sleep he put his sword outside the door. He stayed awake till between two and three o'clock and then called the lad by name.

" 'What do you want from me, master?' says the lad, pulling on his clothes.

" 'My sword I forgot outside the door,' says Fionn, 'and if it rains the rust will ruin it.'

"Out with the lad and he brought in the sword.

" 'Is there anything else you want me to do?' says the lad.

"Fionn said there wasn't. Next day he made off to the old blind man again and told him what had happened.

" 'You have only one more night to catch him,' says the old man, 'and if you fail, he'll be the winner. Try him again at the same time tomorrow night and if he answers you that's the end.'

"Next night Fionn called the lad.

" 'What do you want, master?' says he, jumping up and pulling on his trousers.

"He went to where Fionn was pretending to be snoring.

" 'What did you call me for?'

" 'Did I call you?' says Fionn.

" 'You did.'

" 'It must have been in my sleep,' says Fionn.

"The lad went back. Next day the time was up.

" 'I hope you won't take away any of my power from me,' says Fionn, 'You're the best servant I ever had under my roof.'

" 'I don't want any of your power,' says the lad. 'I never thought of such a thing. All I want is your help to defeat King Cormac.'

" 'Heavens! Why should I do that, and he the king over me? But as I gave you my promise, I'll have to go with you. What day is it to be?'

" 'Any day you choose,' says the lad.

" 'We must give the king time to get his soldiers ready,' says Fionn.

" 'Let it be a month from today then,' says the lad, 'I'll send word to him.'

"The lad went to King Cormac.

" 'As you wouldn't give me the crown of your own free will, I'll take it from you by force,' says he. 'You'll have to fight Fionn Mac Cúil and his army and myself a month from today.'

"And back the lad went to Fionn and stayed with him as before.

" 'You had better go home to your father,' says King Cormac to his young wife a few days before the battle. 'I'll be killed and you too if you stay here.'

"He put his hand in his pocket and pulled out a belt with a yellow plate on it.

" 'Take this belt,' says he, 'and if God sends you a child, and I hope He will, put this belt on him. And when he is able to read what is written on it he'll know who his father was, and I hope he may take revenge on this robber who is taking his place. Come to me on the morning of the battle and I'll give you enough gold and silver to rear the child. I have hidden a boot of gold and one of silver for him in a vessel by the side of that cliff to the east.'

"When the day of battle came the officers and colonels and leading men collected, and the fight began; there was striking and uproar and the blaze of powder, and the screams of men as the bullets pierced them. The smith's daughter went out to see her husband, but she couldn't make him out in the midst of the battle. Cormac was killed and Fionn and his men returned home. Then the leading men in the island of Ireland gathered together and held council, they decided that Cormac's son, as he was called till then, was the heir to the throne. The whole country knew, however, that he wasn't Cormac's son at all. When he became king, he called himself King Conn.

"That was that. The new king began to make new laws, changing everything that was done before. Anyone who couldn't pay the King his rent was sent to prison, and was held there till he paid in some way. Everyone took a hatred and dislike to the King from the moment he took the crown. While King Cormac had reigned the weather was fine, everything was fruitful, and the whole island was a happy place. But the wind changed to the north when King Conn ascended the throne, the land refused to produce crops, summer changed to winter, and the chimneys of the palace became crooked with hatred for the King, and half of them fell down. There was nothing but hardship and slaughter.

"Very well—but wait till you hear! One day the smith's daughter felt that she was about to give birth to a child, and she sent secret word to a midwife that she would like her to accompany her to a lonely place in a certain wood. The midwife came and the pair went to the wood and 'twasn't long till the smith's daughter gave birth to a son.

" 'King Cormac asked me to put this belt on the child, if 'twas a son,' said the mother.

"The midwife put the belt on the child, and no sooner was that done and the child lying on a cloth at their side than out came a wolf from the wood. He bared his teeth and the women fainted, the creatures. He took the child in his teeth and off with him to his cubs in the lair. He never put a tooth in the child but licked him to keep him warm. The wolf had three cubs and suckled them along with the child. When the two women came to their senses, they looked all around but the child was gone and no trace of him.

" 'Don't you pretend a word,' says the smith's daughter to the midwife, putting her hand in her pocket and giving her two guineas. 'Say 'twas something else was wrong with me, and no one will be any the wiser!'

"The wolf guarded the child as if he were the eye in his head, and ended up by being more careful of him than of his own three cubs. The days and weeks and months went by until the child was eighteen months old. On fine days he used to go outside the lair with the cubs and play with them in the wood. One of these days some hunters were passing through the wood with their hounds and horns, or whatever they had at that time, and they caught sight of the three cubs playing with the child on a nice grassy slope. The cubs were more cute than the child and they ran helter-skelter for the lair and hid themselves underground; the child ran after them and escaped too. The hunters thought the whole thing very strange, so they sent word secretly to all who had hounds. Next day they all gathered to watch at the place. When the sun shone out after midday, the wolf left the lair followed by the three cubs, and the child trotting along behind. The play began. The old wolf lay down on his back in the middle of the slope and began to play with his legs with the child, and paid it far more attention than to his own cubs. Then out rushed the hunters with their guns and the attack was on. Off with the hounds after the wolves, but all the hunters wanted was to lay hands on the child. They caught hold of him before he made off to the lair, and he was wild trying to break loose. He wouldn't have long more to live, if they hadn't caught him, for the belt that his mother had put on him the day he was born had sunk into his flesh and was almost hidden. All the hunters began to examine it and read the writing on it.

" 'That's King Cormac's belt, however it came to be on this child!' says they.

"They held council as to who would take the child, and all agreed that he should be given to an old king who lived a long distance away with his queen, who was also old. Cormac Mhac Geolan was this king's name, and he had no children of his own.

"So Cormac Mhac Geolan got the child, and when the old queen saw him she was out of her mind with joy. If 'twas the King of Glory came to her, she couldn't have more welcome for Him! She got a few servants to look after him, and you may be sure that he was the child that got the good care! He grew to be nine or ten years of age, and he had everything he could ask for. He was sent to school to be taught in the manner of the time, and grew to be a strong lad.

"He was so good at the hurling that he beat all the scholars at it one day; the next 'twas the same. He was bigger and stronger than any of them. Now there are always ill-mannered persons in every company, and when the scholars couldn't beat him at the game some of them started to call him a nickname: The Son of the Wolf.

"Next day at school he beat the scholars at hurling and the master as well. The boys and girls and even the master started at the nickname and made a mock of him. Off home with him and left them there and they shouting the name after him as hard as they could.

" 'I know they have some reason for it,' says he, 'even the master was saying it, and he wouldn't if it wasn't true. I won't stay here another day or night,' says he to Cormac Mhac Geolan, 'except you tell me what it is all about.'

" 'Very well, I'll tell you,' says Cormac Mhac Geolan. 'We found you as a child in the woods, playing with a wolf and her three cubs, and the hunters left you here for me to rear as my heir. As you see for yourself you're the only one to take it.'

" 'Had I any clothes or anything on me when I was found?' says the lad.

" 'Not a thing, but like you came into the world,' says Cormac Mhac Geolan, 'except for a small belt you had on.'

" 'Where is the belt?'

"Cormac Mhac Geolan had the belt ahide in a chest in the room. He went down to the room for it and gave it to the lad. He read the writing on the plate, that he was a son to King Cormac.

" 'Now I know that I'm no son of a wolf but the son of a good man, King Cormac,' says he, 'and if I'm alive tomorrow morning, I'll be taking my leave of ye for a while till I find out how things are where my father used to live.'

"Well, the next morning the old queen got ready a good meal for him, and she crying at the thought that he was leaving them. Cormac Mhac Geolan went up to the lad and handed him a big purse of gold.

" 'Put that in your pocket,' says he. 'You might need it before you come back.'

"He said goodbye to Cormac Mhac Geolan and the old queen, and set off for the road early that morning. He didn't know the way so he asked people here and there where King Cormac used to live. The evening got very cold. The lad saw a big fence of bushes by the roadside and a small house a bit behind it. There was a small, old man herding a few sheep by the road, and who was he but Gaibhne Gow, his grandfather.

" 'You wouldn't happen to know,' says the lad to him, 'where hereabouts used King Cormac live?'

" 'I'll show you the place,' says the old man, and the tears in his eyes. 'That's his palace to the west there on the brow of the hill, but he's dead himself for the past twenty years. His place was taken by a thief that doesn't let us in peace day or night since he put the crown on his head.'

"He went down to the room with the old man and they ate a tasty meal. When they had eaten enough the young lad pulled out the bottle and gave two glasses to the old man. He sat at the table chatting with the youngest daughter and smoking his pipe, and he put his two arms to the back of his head to stretch himself—you have often seen people do that—and the buckle of his belt was exposed. The girl recognized it the minute she laid eyes on it, and she started to cry. The old man had left them alone.

" 'If 'tis how you don't want to have me here till morning,' says the young lad, 'I'll go to some other house.'

" 'Oh it isn't that at all!' says the girl, ' 'Tis the name on the belt you are wearing.'

" 'How do you recognize my belt?' says he.

" 'I was married to King Cormac for a short while before he was killed,' says she, 'and he gave me that belt and told me if I gave birth to a son to put the belt on him so that he would know who his father was. I went to the wood, and when my son was born I put the belt on him. And then a wolf took him off and I haven't had trace or tidings of him since. But that's the belt. How did you get it?'

" 'Now I know!' says the lad. 'You're my mother and I'm in my own home!'

"The girl was wild with joy, and she told the news to the rest.

" 'Where's your father?' says the young lad.

"She called him in and the young lad filled out two other glasses and gave them to him. They started to talk and the old man told about how wicked King Conn was. Every night someone had to sit up with him telling him stories and anyone he didn't like or who wasn't to his satisfaction was shot or hanged in the morning. It was the old man's turn to go that night.

" 'So that's the way!' says the young lad. 'I myself will see tonight what he is like,' says he.

"When the lad entered the palace, he turned into the kitchen. The servants were eating their supper round a table, and none of them moved to offer a bite to the stranger. He went over to the table boldly and sat down like the others. The servants looked at one another, making out that he had no manners at seating himself without being invited.

" 'As I'm going to spend the night here, the least I ought to get is a bite of food,' says the lad.

"When the cooks heard that, they put food and drink that had the flavor of honey in front of him, and no two bites or no two sups had the one taste. The cook that was getting the king's meal ready for him came in and told the lad that the King wanted him. He went in.

" 'I don't seem to know you,' says the King.

" 'I'm a stranger here,' says the lad. 'I'm staying in a house down there with an old man and his three daughters. The old man told me you had sent for him to come and tell you stories till morning, but he got sick after dinner today and I took pity on him and said I'd come in his stead.'

" 'Very well,' says the King.

"You could see your reflection on everything in the room where the King was lying. There was a fine fire and comfortable chairs round about. The King himself was lying on a bed of feathers by the fireside.

" 'Start off now,' says the King, 'and tell me the best stories you have.'

"He turned his face to the wall and covered his head with the clothes. When day was breaking next morning, he turned around on his side in the bed.

" 'You're the best storyteller that ever came to my palace,' says he to the lad.

" 'But you didn't hear half of what I was saying,' says the lad.

" 'There wasn't a word you said that I didn't hear,' says the king.

" 'How is that? Weren't you asleep half the time?'

" 'I wasn't,' said the King. 'I haven't closed an eye in sleep for seven years or maybe twice seven.'

" 'Then you must have some of the otter's nature in you,' says the lad.

" 'Don't let me hear you saying that again!' says the King, with a touch of anger.

" 'All I say is that you couldn't have heard all I was telling you,' says the lad.

" 'No word escaped my ears,' says the King; 'and,' says he, rising up on his elbow, 'don't let me hear mention of an otter from your lips again!'

" 'Is your mother living?' says the lad.

" 'She is.'

" 'Go to her then and ask her how you came into the world!'

"The King jumped out on the floor, and off with him through the palace till he reached the bed where his mother was asleep. He shook her by the arm.

" 'Mother,' says he, 'how did I come into the world?'

" 'How would you come into the world, my son,' says she, 'but as the child of King Cormac?'

" 'Well, what did she say?' asked the lad of the King.

" 'That I was King Cormac's son,' said he.

"The King went back to bed and pulled the clothes over his head, and the lad began to tell more stories to him. After a long while, the King spoke again.

" 'You are the best storyteller I have ever listened to in this palace,' said he.

" 'You can't have been listening to them all,' replied the lad.

" 'Haven't I told you already that I heard every word of them?'

" 'Then you must be a half-otter,' said the lad again.

" 'If you say that again, I'll put your head rolling round the floor,' said the King, seizing hold of the sword beside his bed.

" 'Come, come!' said the lad, 'I have a sword too,' drawing his sword from his side. 'Take your sword back to your mother's bed-side,' said he to the King. 'Take hold of her by the throat, put her across your knee at the edge of the bed and point the sword at her breast, and swear that you'll drive it through her except she tells you the truth about your father.'

"The King rushed back to his mother's room, caught hold of her by the throat, dragged her to the edge of the bed and pressed the point of the sword against her bosom.

" 'Now, tell me the truth about how I was got!' he screamed.

"His mother knew by him that he was in earnest and she grew terrified of him. So she told him all about how she and her sisters had been out on the lake and how the otter had caught up with her.

" 'That's the true story of how you came,' said she. 'You are no son to King Cormac.'

" 'I understand,' said King Conn. 'I had suspicions about myself. That lad has got me the truth at last.'

"When he returned to the lad, he took him by the two hands and threw himself on his knees, asking his pardon.

" 'I nearly committed a murder,' said King Conn. 'Now I know that you were telling me the truth.'

"The King drew on his clothes and sat down to chat calmly and peaceably with the young lad.

" 'I can get you the power of sleeping by this day week,' said the lad.

" 'If you do, I'll promise you in writing half of my wealth indoors and outside, and my throne after my death,' said Conn.

" 'Write the promise,' said the lad, 'and I'll quickly do the rest.'

"The King wrote the promise.

" 'Haven't you got good boats in your harbors?' asked the lad.

" 'I have,' said the King.

" 'Well, take one of them and attach a chain to it, long enough to let it out into the middle of the lake below the palace. Tie the other end of the chain at the lakeshore. Bring your bed of feathers out into the boat, and cover the boat so that the rain won't get through. I promise you that you'll quickly sleep, if you do that.'

"And so it was done. The King got ready a boat, with his feather bed in it and a cover on top. He tied a chain from the boat to the shore. And when all was ready King Conn entered the boat and lay down on the bed. The boat drifted on the waves till it was out as far as the chain allowed. The King fell fast asleep the moment he lay down over the water and never woke for three days and nights, but snored with all his might as if he would never get enough sleep.

"What was in the lake but the otter! He got the smell of a human being and rose up by night and entered the boat. He dragged out the sleeping King, pulled him under the water and killed him. When the servants thought that the King had slept enough they pulled in the boat by the chain, but there was no trace of the King to be found. Then the searching started and they dragged the lake with crooks. They found the King's body at the bottom; the otter had taken off his head. There was great lamentation as his body was taken in and waked and buried.

"King Conn's mother was living in the palace and the lad went to her and told her that he had the King's promise in writing that the lands and palace and throne would be his after Conn's death.

" 'If it is your wish,' said he, 'we will let the counselors decide. I will let you have whatever they agree upon.'

"The leading men and lawyers gathered. The lad showed them

the writing of the King, promising him the throne after his death. Orders were given to all the servants in the palace to leave. The lad was crowned, and became King instead of Conn. He sent for Cormac Mhac Geolan and his queen who had reared him, and invited them to live with him. He also brought his grandfather and his mother's two sisters, and sent an invitation to the four corners of his kingdom; rich and poor collected, and a feast was held, the like of which was never before in Ireland. The tenants were overjoyed at having a young King over them. And that's how King Conn met his end in my story, and how the son of King Cormac took his place."

Sean took up his pipe from the table where he had laid it. He stared at it. Then he stared at Séamus Delargy and at me. "That story is as true as you're alive," he said.

"But I suppose now," said Tadhg, "that the creatures of the water, not being able to sleep, I suppose that they wouldn't be tormented in themselves the way you and I would be lying awake at night."

"I don't know then," said Sean. "But them that was that way enchanted in human form suffered everything that you or I would suffer if we lay awake for years. And worse. Or so the old people used to tell me. And the seal above the others, Tadhg, you know well, for they say she is something differing from every creature."

"They do say she's a kind of a fairy," said Tadhg.

"Well, myself I never remarked anything unnatural in the seal. I've heard things said of her. I've known men that wouldn't go near her to kill her, and men that would cross themselves looking at the dead body of her. But myself and my father were close to them all our lives. And I myself have handled them alive and dead, as you know, Tadhg. And I never yet saw any harm come from them—nor did my father before me, God have mercy on his soul."

Sean crossed himself.

I said, "It was your trade then, killing seals when you were young?"

"The last man I went sealing with," said Sean, "was a man called Tadhg the Tooth. A Murphy man he was. His name was Murphy and all the latter part of his life when I knew him he had only the one tooth. It was he used to go killing seals with my father. It was into the cave they went those times for seals—into the darkness of the cave on the headland above the house here. And a big crowd of men used to go there together. They used to leave their boats outside at the mouth of the cave and swim in there with every man a flaming torch of bog deal stuck in his hat to give him light. Every man had a mattock for to strike the seals and kill them, and every man carried a stocking filled with black fire coals for to throw to the seals when they were angered."

"Oh, they did, they did," said Tadhg. "But myself I heard it was in the sleeves of their coats they put the burnt coals."

"Some put them in their sleeves, and some in their trouser legs."

"They did," said Tadhg Tracy, "for they knew that if a seal caught a hold of you she wouldn't be satisfied with squeezing you until she heard the bones cracking, and if she heard the coals cracking she'd let go her hold thinking 'twas the bone."

"That's right," said Sean. "That's what I say. But some believed it was safer to carry the coals in a stocking and throw that before them to the seals. Anyway the Murphy man went one day to the seal cave by himself. And he tied his boat to the rock outside and he swam in, with his mattock, this stocking of burned coals slung about his neck and his lighted torch stuck in his hat. But you must understand how when a crowd of men swam in together the flickering of ten or twelve torches on the water would give a good light up and down, and a man might be in good heart with that, seeing his comrades about him and they maybe calling one to another; but when Tadhg the Tooth swam in alone he saw before him just the one small glimmer, and the waves about him were washing hollow in his ears. And when he reached the little pebble strand at the far end of the cave, and stood there on his two feet to look about him, he heard the moaning of the seal. Now that is a mournful sound when you hear it outside on the wind, and though I am well used to it myself, living here above the seal caves all my life, it has put the heart across me many times when I'd be alone at night. It is the most lonely cry in the world. But if it tears hard at you outside in the open, when you hear it suddenly, and you alone with the echo of the cave and the dark water lapping, then you'd be inclined to pray to God and go home. Tadhg the Tooth made a start to turn back, but the seal, as he turned, came toward him over the pebbled strand. It was narrow where she lay, you understand, between two rocks, and when she saw him there she was mad with fear and she thought her nearest chance was to pass by him and go for the water. But if she did, wasn't he afraid she would attack his legs, and he threw to her the stocking of coals, and there she lay crunching them a minute. So he hit her well on the nose with his mattock and she left off her hold and lay dead.

"She was a big seal, but Tadhg was strong and he looked at her and looked at the water, and the only way he could see to shift her was to fix a line of rope about her and roll her before him till he put her in the water. When he had her floated he held on to the line with one hand and started to swim. But now the tide was against him and with one hand useless he had no strength against the water and he thought he would never win out. So back again he came to where he could stand with the water about his middle, and by this he was desperately cold and his clothes tight against him, and the torch on his head was giving out. And he could hear the howling of a bull seal in the echo of the cave above.

"So then he tied the end of the line around his neck and with two hands free for swimming he made way against the tide. But halfways out, where the turn of the cave is, at the place where you get your first blink of daylight coming out, what does she do but come alive. The water put life into her, do you see? It often happened that way, when you thought your seal was dead. And soon 'twas how the seal was pulling Tadhg, instead of he pulling her. She pulled him down. She pulled him twice down under the water, and as you know well no man can swim against a seal. So now Tadhg was like a salmon giving line and taking line this way and that against the play of a rod for many minutes. And whenever he gained a piece of slack against the seal he made to loosen the knot he had tied around his neck, but every time he was too late. She drew it tight again and drew him under. Well, what do you think he did then? He put line against the one tooth he had and he cut it strand by strand till at the next bold dive the seal made the line broke and Tadhg was free. They called him Tadhg the Tooth after that. That's how he got his name. Because only for his one tooth being good, the seal had him drowned."

"What made you stop sealing?" I asked him, after a while.

"It was my father's trade, but he died, as I was telling you, soon after my mother, before I was twenty years of age—and I had to mind the house and bit of land here for the brothers and sisters. And at that time, too, there was this landlord I was telling you about—a man most constantly set against the killing of the seals."

"Yes. Yes," said Tadhg, as though he didn't want to hear any more.

"Well, several parties came over to the house from time to time looking for a drop of seal oil. It was a great cure, you know, Tadhg, and is yet, for all kinds of sprains and rheumatism and one thing and another like that. And the people here used to get it from my father, so they did expect the same from me after his death. And I didn't like to disappoint them—although to tell the truth I had enough and more to do at home without that part of my father's business on the top of it. However, they'd be sending word, and sending word for seal oil, and some of them walking down from the mountains only to find me without a drop for them. So I made up my mind to get a seal and satisfy them. So out with me one morning with the gun, for I thought I'd best get one in the daylight on the strand below the cliff. I thought to myself, you know, that it would be easier on myself to get one that way, rather than go into the cave with the boat and get one there—myself single-handed with the boat and a dead seal in the darkness of the cave. So out with me then, and who did I meet but the landlord himself.

" 'Good morning,' says he.

" 'Good morning, sir,' says I. ' 'Tis a grand sunny day,' says I. 'I thought to get a rabbit,' says I, 'on a sunny day like this—something for to give the children to their dinner.'

" 'I see,' says the landlord, and he looks at me. 'Well, Sean,' says he, 'I see the world is upside down.'

" 'There's no harm, I hope, sir,' says I, 'if I go and get a rabbit for the children to their dinner.'

" 'There's no harm in that, Sean,' says he, 'but there's harm in it surely,' says he, 'when the rabbits leave the hill and go down to the edge of the water,' says he. 'They'll likely next be feeding off the sea-weed,' says he, 'and you making your way over the sands at low tide for to shoot them.'

" 'I thought to get one on the top of the cliff,' says I. 'I saw a dozen of them feeding there last evening.'

" 'And tell me this,' says the landlord to me: 'Did you ever see them feeding there at noon on a hot summer's day?'

" 'I did not, sir!'

" 'And what time is it now?'

" 'About noon, sir.'

" 'About noon on a hot summer's day.'

"That was the last he said to me. And from that I knew well that he knew I was after the seals. So I just took a little walk for myself by the edge o' the cliff. And I saw two big seals lying there below on the strand. But I left them where they lay and went home. I thought it all out in the night, how I could get this seal, and the only time, God forgive me, that I knew I was safe from the landlord was on a Sunday morning when he would be at Mass. So I planned all well for that time. I took my gun out by night, on the Saturday night, and I hid it underneath the clump of furze bushes that was growing by the cliff. And on the Sunday morning I put on my suit the same as usual as though to go to Mass. And I walked out away from the chapel up the road toward the point where I thought to myself I'd meet no one, mine being the last house out, the same as you see it today. And I walked on and the day was bright. And who did I meet but the landlord again himself.

" 'Good morning,' says he. 'So you're walking away from Mass this morning,' he says.

" 'Good morning sir,' says I, and the funny thing was I was think-ing nearly the same way about him as he was thinking about me — wondering to myself how he was so far off from his own right road to Mass. But I thought to myself 'It is well I'm not carrying the gun,' and I wasn't so much afraid as the first time.

"So I told him I had a cousin married in the next parish, and that I had it in mind to go and see her that day. And I said if I took the cliff road and cut across the bog beyond I would reach that other chapel well in time for second Mass and see my cousin after.

" 'Well, Sean,' says he, 'you're a good man and I hope your cousin's grateful when she sees the long road you took to see her.'

" 'I'll think I'll find it quicker than the other road,' says I.

" 'The quickest road is the road your mind is set on,' says he, and he went on to Mass.

"When I knew it was safe I slipped down the path between the cliffs to the strand. There's a big rock there, and coming up quietly, I lay behind it to use it as a hide. I saw five seals lying there, four cows and a bull. The bull lay nearest to me and he was a big one, but I saw nothing at the time to remark in the way his coat was spotted. I shot him fair and he was dead before the others reached the water's edge. Well, I had a long job before me then, and a small space of time for it, to get it done before Mass would be over. I had to go for the horse and the ropes and make him fast and haul him up the path of the cliff and along the road to the house here.

"Well, I left the skinning until after nightfall, and I never saw the landlord more for a week. But when I was skinning this seal I did take notice of a white mark he had on him by the side of his neck, a strange shape of a mark, like three links of a chain. There was not more than six inches in the whole of it, and you never would remark it unless you looked close. So anyways I thought nothing about it, only to look at it once. And I hung the skin behind the house here, and I got the big stones and the pans that hadn't been used since my father fell sick of the fever, and I put the blubber between them to press the oil out. And some of the meat I brought into the house and cooked it for the children. Did you ever taste the meat of the seal?"

"I did not," said Tadhg, "but I once smelt it."

"I was sore afraid of the smell in case maybe the landlord would pass and find me out. But it wasn't that way he found me. It wasn't

until the week was over that I met him again, and this time it was
after Mass at our own chapel. He rode his horse beside me a piece
of the way home.

" 'Sean,' says he, 'I have lost one of my seals.' That's what he said
to me.

" 'I beg your pardon, sir,' says I.

" 'I think it's one of the bulls,' says the landlord, 'and I'm beginning to think he's come to some harm.'

" 'I understand, sir,' says I.

" 'It's a week since I saw him,' says the landlord, looking at me
very straight. 'As a matter of fact it was on a Sunday on the way to
Mass, just before meeting you, I saw this seal.'

"I took a bit of courage then, and 'I'm not sure but you might be
mistaken, sir,' says I, 'for no man can count the seals in the sea.'

" 'You think not,' says the landlord.

" 'It would be a hard job surely.'

" 'Everyone of them is different,' says the landlord. 'I would
know them apart as well as you would know your own brothers and
sisters one from another. And I know when one of them is missing
as well as you would know if your brother was missing.'

"I said nothing to that.

" 'Well you don't believe me, Sean,' says the landlord.

" 'I do believe you surely,' says I, 'but the sea is big and the seal
cave itself is dark, with great numbers of seals lying in it.'

" 'Well now,' says the landlord to me, 'you would know your own
cattle and your sheep, would you not?'

" 'I would.'

" 'No matter if you had a hundred or two hundred of them—and
you'd be able to go in among them at night and pick out those you
wanted for the fair in the morning.'

" 'I would, of course, sir. Any man could do that, with his own.'

" 'Well, Sean,' says he, 'I know my own seals—them that have
their living in the seal cave at the Point beyond—I know them the
very same as you would know your beasts.'

" 'To do that,' says I, 'you'd nearly need to count them, the same as a man would count his beasts.'

" 'And I do count them, Sean,' says he. 'Will you believe me that? And I am very grieved that this old bull is gone—he was one that had a mark on him, Sean. He had a white mark like three links of a chain by the side of his neck.'

"What would you do, Tadhg," said Sean, "if you found yourself facing a landlord like that?"

"You couldn't well hope to hide what you'd done."

"You could not. Well, I went home. But I had it so on my mind I couldn't rest. Day nor night I couldn't feel easy, until on the third day I went over to the landlord's house and I told him it was I shot the seal."

"And what did he say?" asked Tadhg.

"He said nothing first, only looked at me the same as before. Then I asked him would I bring him the skin, and he shouted at me then. 'Go home out of this!' he said."

"Did you hear more about it?"

"Never a word. He never spoke a word to me from that day. And I never shot another seal since."

Sean, as his way had been, I suppose, ever since he grew too old for work, began and finished all he had to do or say by attending to his pipe. It was one thing at a time with him now, smoking or talking, walking or talking. The pipe had gone out, so he filled it and took up from the fire a glowing piece of turf to light it with. He put a wind shield on the pipe. He climbed up to the loft and came down with a piece of wire. He stuck the wire through the burning turf and twisted its end into a hook, and with that hanging from his heavy fist he led the way outside.

The moon was bright on the sea, like a river flowing inland toward us, and out of the hillside it scooped black hollows deeper than any you could see by day.

We stopped at a turn in the road for Sean to say, "It was here I met the landlord and he going to Mass." Then we climbed to the point above the seal place. "It was there below to the west that Tadhg the Tooth swam ashore."

As we stood and watched the sea we heard a sound of wailing, distant and soon gone, leaving an echo in my mind like notes of a lament impossible to remember, like the sobbing of a girl in a dark house of many rooms—but how to find her unless she sobs again?—and like a snatch of an ancient modal song. I looked at Sean.

"That's one of them," he said. "It is a lonely sound. If you climb this wall and go down the slope of the grass, you'll likely see her sitting on the rock or below in the water, the creature. But watch the cliff's edge for there's a place or two there where the land is rotten."

At the cliff's edge we saw nothing but black rock and the moonlight on the waves, and Sean said. "It's a wonder she's not there. Not herself, nor the bull. In the old days, would you believe it, I have seen a hundred seals below there at the mouth of the cave gathered like children out of school. You will see one or two now in the moonlight if you wait and watch. One or two is the most you will see for there is nothing now the way it was the old times. The land hasn't the people working on it, nor the hill the sheep, nor cattle that it had; nor the sea hasn't the strong shoals of herring in it, nor the mackerel, nor none of the creatures that were, only a few old ones stuck here and there like myself. Lie down for yourself there and watch the water and I'll go and see if I can rouse them."

He walked back over the grass, following what he knew to be the course of the cave below him. He picked up a large stone. In the moonlight one could see a black hollow near him in the grass and into this he threw the stone. It echoed and fell, and fell.

You could see no movement in the water as the seal swam out, but after a few minutes his round head appeared and he looked in our direction toward the entrance of the cave, a round head gazing steadily, a black blob one minute, an old man's head next. He gazed for a while, then sank with no sound. He came up later with another head beside him, and until the clouds covered the moon an hour later we lay and watched the sea and watched these two as they came to the surface and stared, went down again and rose silently in another place.

"Is it fear that makes them gaze at their cave?"

"Maybe the noise of that stone is in their heads. And maybe they know better than you or me how 'twas only a stone from above, but there's nothing to be had by looking for the minds of those creatures."

"I just wondered if they were watching for something to come out of the cave."

He blew on his piece of turf until it burned red in the darkness and he held it up to his pipe. We stared at the seals and sometimes imagined they stared at us, but it was impossible in the moonlight to see their eyes. Very still, they floated, rising and falling with the gentle waves, their bodies upright in the water, as I am told. I was thinking of the seal in the salmon bothy when Sean spoke again.

"And if they are gazing this way, they are gazing south," he said. "And south is for Good." It is the same word in Irish. "North is for Evil. There is no good ever came out of the north."

"And east and west?"

"East is before you and west is at the back of you. But what is in the mind of them, I don't know—the creatures."

THERE IS A VILLAGE KNOWN TO THE POOR TRAVELING
people of Ireland as "Baile an ghrá Dia," the village of the Love of
God, or if you like, the charitable place, for the Irish name for char-
ity is "Love of God." It was there that I first heard stories of good
deeds done by seals. The village is on the north coast of Mayo, in
poor and isolated country, so poor and isolated that the beggars and
poor traveling people and the wandering storytellers used to come
there in their hundreds, knowing they were sure of food and of a
place to sleep by the fire. They were valued as strangers, for their
voices or their talents or for the news they brought, and even now if
you meet a North Mayo man on the road you should be willing to
tell him of your purpose.

I had three or four miles to walk and once I stopped to look at a
cairn of stones by the roadside. Out of a hole in the ground about
fifty yards away, where he was cutting turf, a man came slowly to me.

"It's a nice day," I said.

"It is grand drying weather, thanks be to God."

"Can you tell me the way to the ferry?"

"I can surely." He gave me a direct and open look with the distant
eyes that seamen often have. His were dark.

"You are a stranger?"

"Yes."

"I was thinking that when I saw you by the leacht."

"I was wondering whether I had the right road."

"No fear of that. There's only the one road till you come to the cross. You'll be from Ballina, is it? You got off the bus above?"

"I had a lift in a lorry, so far."

"You'll be from Dublin, maybe?"

"I stayed there a while, but really I'm from London."

"From London? Dear, dear. I was thinking you were English. You have a kind of an English accent, do you know. Well, you're welcome, and if it's the ferry you're wanting I'll show you a piece of the road down. You're on your holidays, are you? Have you the wife with you? Will she come by the bus?"

"No, I'm not married."

"That's strange. Well maybe you'll find yourself a nice Mayo girl. Now most of the Englishmen I met were married, for there's plenty of money over there I believe. Plenty of money in England, and you never saw such land, so there's nothing to stop any Englishman marrying young."

"I suppose they do marry younger over there, but most of them live in the towns, you see."

"That's right."

"And they don't have to think about what land they'll have, and there's very little business over dowries and all that. No farm to be thought of—only what wages you earn from some job, and somewhere to live if you can find it."

"There's not enough houses, I heard."

"Some people get married and go to live in one room."

"Dear me. I waited sixteen years for my house before I was married. But I think in England there's little heed taken of these things. There's little respect in England for the living or the dead. I was there many times at the harvest and I knew several of them, good and decent in every way to talk to, but I knew one, and would you believe this, I knew his wife well for he'd bring me home with him now and again for tea, and a fine strong woman she was, but didn't she die, and will you believe this—didn't he have her burned with fire. And he did love her I believe."

"Yes. It's not unusual there."

"It was in childbirth she died and the baby died after. And 'twas the same for the baby—burned with fire."

"I suppose that seems a terrible thing to you."

"It does. When I think it could be one of my own. Now there couldn't be the like of a graveyard for such a thing. Not so much as a stone to mark the place, I suppose."

"I think the ashes are usually scattered in a garden and then there's a little plaque put up on the wall of the chapel, or some place like that."

"But a person could never find the place where the burial was. Tell me this, would they not put a cross in the ground by the marks of the fire, or build some small leacht, itself?"

"Some have a tree planted in the place where the ashes were strewn—but there's no fire outside, you know. It's done in a building in a special furnace."

"I understand."

"What is a leacht, then?"

"You are standing by one now."

I looked at the cairn of loose stones, and remembered how, when I last saw one like it, I had found by its side a red flannel rag.

"It is more than a hundred years old, this leacht beside you now, and it marks the place where one died on the road—by the name of Michael Sean, a great-great-uncle of mine. It was the custom to build these stones where a person was found dead abroad in the open; and where a coffin was laid by the side of the road, on the way to the burial, there it was the custom to build the leacht too. It isn't right to leave the coffin down, but sometimes it will happen. It was our way too for any person passing to put a stone on the heap and to say a prayer, but only a few old people now remember to do that."

"Why is it wrong to put the coffin down?"

"It's not right. But from here to the graveyard is the longest road you'll find, down along to the cross, the way you'll be walking now, and turn there to the ferry below, and at the ferry then you'll bring the coffin on the boat and away up the creek to the shore beyond."

"And how did your uncle die in this spot?"

"Nobody knew because he was then at the height of his strength—a powerful worker—and a man I dare say as big as myself, working just the same as you see me at the bog, and at the fishing and at his garden of land year in year out. But he died here some time in the evening and there was no one passing until the next day, when an old traveling woman met him and he lying dead across the bank with his hat tumbled down in the center of the road. They do say he had warning one year before. It was this same traveling woman that did warn him."

"What kind of a warning?"

"She was the kind that has knowledge."

He left his work and came with me two miles down the hill road to the ferry. As we came to the first low house of that straggling village we could hear the sea pounding, but did not see it until we were close at a ridge where the road sloped steeply down to a narrow quay. Beside the quay stood the ferry house only three or four yards from the sea.

"Will we row across now?" said the man from the bog.

"Well, is the ferryman here? I was told to see the ferryman. That's really what I came for."

"I understand."

"Is it here he lives? In this house?"

"That's my house—yes."

"Oh, I see. I'm sorry I . . . "

"Yes, I'm the man you're looking for—Michael the Ferry they call me. I thought maybe when you asked me the road to the ferry, it was how you wanted to go across. And this boy is my child. Come over to me here, Mickeen."

A barefooted boy with wild hair ran toward us, stopped, and ran to hide behind the house.

"He's that way with a stranger."

"Yes."

"But if he sees me go for the boat he'll be before us. Will you go over now?"

"What is there over there?"

"Just what you see. Those few houses and the chapel and the pub, and beyond to the south there, about a mile, the graveyard. Look there now, and you'll see where it is. You see where the strand is yellow over there; that place is called the Beach of the Seals, and above it the green bank and a bit of a wall. Follow that along south a bit, south, and there where the sun is striking now on something white. That white glint, that's a white stone. That's the newest headstone there. That is over the grave of Nuala, my wife, God be good to her. That will show you where the graveyard lies."

"I am sorry. How long ago was it?"

"Two months. She would be forty-five years on next November Day, if God did spare her."

"Had she a long illness?"

"Not at all, 'twas with the baby. And he's a grand, strong baby, I thank God. And it's a fine woman that nursed him. It is she who looks after the house now and the other children."

"How many others have you?"

"Five with the baby. The boy there is the oldest."

He took up the oars that were lying by the wall of the house and threw them into the boat. As we came down the steps of the quay the boy splashed through the water from the shore and climbed into the boat before us. A gull screamed. The boy jumped up on the stern and waved his arms and screamed back at it as it circled. He mimicked it so well that we both laughed.

Michael said, "You don't understand him, do you?"

"How do you mean?"

"You have no Irish?"

"No."

As we pulled away from the shore he looked at Mickeen and laughed.

"What is it the sea gull says, Mickeen?"

Mickeen made the sound again and this time it seemed to be a rhyme.

"And what does he say in English?"

"The sea gull has no English."

"Maybe. But if he had English, what would he say then?"

"He'd say, 'Keep it together.' He'd say, 'Fish,' but it would be useless, Da, it wouldn't rhyme."

"Never mind would it rhyme or not," said Michael, pulling on the oars. "What would he say?"

"He'd say, 'Fish, fish, fish. Keep it together. Don't share it.' Then he'd say, 'Fish, fish, fish. Food for the king.' "

"That's about what it means," said Michael to me.

And Mickeen said, "But when the sea gull talks in English his mother doesn't know what he's at."

"Is that so?"

"How would she? Fish, fish, fish—whoever heard a sea gull talk like that?"

"We had a rhyme for every bird when I was his age, and some of the animals too, and every one had the right sound to it."

He made a harsh sound broken into gaps of two syllables. "What is it the grouse says, Mickeen?"

"You're after saying it. Say it again."

"But in English what does he say?"

"Sure I know what it is in English, Da."

"When he's feeding on the moor he says, 'Spare the heather, spare the heather, spare the heather.' That's what the cock says to the hen. And she says to him again, 'Do you see on that hill and that hill and that other hill, the heather still to be eaten?' And the cock says back to her, 'Can't you see that cow, and that cow, and that other cow eating it?'

"And the cat? And the cat! What does she say? The cat—oh look at him, Da! Oh look at the seal!"

"Do you think he will win against the current?"

"He's a big one."

"He's losing way. I did think I found it heavy on the oars."

"Well it must be a terrible tide when it's too strong for that one— oh look at him, Da! Did you ever see one bigger?"

It had been the custom, Michael told me, for the ferrymen to watch the seals and so judge the speed of the tide as it races through this channel. By keeping near the shore, we gained on the current, and on the seal, and fell back fast to a sandy promontory on the opposite shore. The seal swam slowly and after a while turned away to the open sea.

"Some days you are not able to come over with the boat. You can tell, when you see what trouble that creature is in, the strength that's in this tide, for the seal is the swiftest swimmer in the sea; herself, the ray and the mackerel. An odd one or two like the one you see there will swim up this narrow place after the salmon and they'll chase them up the river too—a good bit up. But when there's no salmon about and the seals are here by the ferry you know there's bad weather before you. A storm out beyond will drive them in. They will have knowledge of a storm before it breaks and then they'll lie close to the shore, or lie in to a creek. But there is nothing you can learn by looking at them only, the way you might look at a stranger's boat lying this way or that way on the water. You must study them to know are they lying in for play or for fish, or in the autumn time for mating. For they do like to mate in shallow pools, or by the sea's edge somewhere. Or are they looking to the weather and the tides. And I believe there's few men can watch them rightly. But I can. And this boy can, and every man of the ferry can, for five generations back, which is the time my family held the ferry. We were always on good terms with the seals and close to them, and even in the old times, when you might win as much by killing a seal as now you would killing a pig, no man of the ferry would molest them. Those men that did, and some made their living by it, had no luck after. Indeed, I have heard my grandfather say, 'It is better to have nothing to do with seals unless you are willing to do well by them.' "

The boy stayed by the boat and we went up to the public house where I was to find lodging. Like so many Irish public houses, it sold clothes, rabbit snares, groceries and ploughshares, and you sat and had your drinks in a dark corner at the back. There were three or four men in there talking, and we sat by them on the barrels. It was not until two hours later when Michael the Ferryman got up to go that I knew they were waiting for his boat. The two hours started like this.

Michael said, "I was telling this man about the Cregans."

"What were you telling me?" I said.

"That is to say I was to tell you the next minute."

"Well there's two of them here," said the man in the corner. "There's Joseph Tom Cregan and myself, I'm Patrick Sean."

"And isn't it true," said Michael, "that no Cregan was ever drowned?"

"It is true, and the Cregans were a great fishing family in days gone by."

"You are yet."

"But there's not the fishing in it, now, that there was in the time of the old Cregans that lived in the village of Altmore. Well, they say in those times there was no man could handle a boat like a Cregan, because a Cregan had no fear at all, and where the other fishermen of Altmore might lie ashore in wild weather a Cregan would put out and he'd get fish too when the sea looked impossible to all. And no matter how many times the men ashore would lose hope for them, they would surely come home safe. The old people used to say it was the fairies made them that way against drowning."

"Is that so then?" said Michael. "For I heard it was the seals."

"No. No, the time o' the seal came after."

A voice in the darkness said, "But isn't she supposed to be a kind of fairy anyway? She's under some kind of an enchantment, I heard them say."

"She's not like other creatures," said Michael. "But I heard it was a seal that saved the Cregans."

"Oh it was, it was. It was a seal on one occasion. But the gift the Cregans had was older than that—much older. It was there long years before the occasion of the seal. And the reason for it was supposed to be that one Cregan many years ago did some great good to the fairies."

" 'Twas the same thing with the seal—they did good to the seal," said Michael.

"That is so."

"There was five of them in the boat," said Michael. "Five Cregan men from Altmore, and they fishing with nets from a curragh, a little way off their own coast. And 'twas a heavy day and close, like as if it would thunder, but no sign that any of them saw of a powerful storm just a ground swell and little wind when first they put out. But when the wind came it came suddenly off shore and a big storm was at them before they knew. So they made to row for the shore. But the sea and wind were against them and night came and they were exhausted, till, in the darkness of the night, they were driven out to sea further and further. And with no landmarks, nor no stars in the sky, they did not know which way to head. So they lay as best they could until morning keeping the head of the curragh into the sea. And when the day came there was no sight of land nor ship. And the second day the same. And they were exhausted with cold, and having no food, only the raw fish from their nets, the hunger came on them sorely. They took the fish and sat on it to warm it before they went to eat.

"On the third day they thought they must be somewhere out in the North Atlantic many miles from land and they were rowing southeastward, as well as they could judge by the sun, when one of them saw a seal rise up between the waves near to them. They were delighted with the seal. They threw fish to him. They had plenty of fish in the nets. And every now and again they threw him another one. He was swimming on a different course from theirs, but they made up their minds to follow him. And follow him they did for above an hour. But a seal swims fast, and the five Cregan men were destroyed, until with their hunger and exhaustion there was none of them able to pull an oar at all. They lay back and they knew they were lost. The seal was gone and they never saw him again. Now the people of Altmore were full sure by this that the five Cregan men were lost, and the wake was held, and all the village mourned them for dead."

"It's a terrible thing," said a slow voice somewhere, "to be at a wake and no corpse."

"Five of them gone and no corpse," said the man in the corner.

"Well, how many days would you hold back the wake before you were sure?" said the slow voice.

" 'Twould depend on the tides—the whole village would be searching, in below the cliff for several days maybe."

"But anyway," said Michael, "there was no corpse found."

"And I do believe," said the man in the corner, "they held the wake back a full fortnight or more. Because no one would believe a Cregan could be drowned. 'Twas the priest in the end that told them to wake the five men."

"The wake when they did hold it was two days and two nights and, there being five, it was a great wake, more drink and food than at any wake ever and every kind of story told at it and every game played by the mourners. Well it happened while the men were trying their strength, one against the other, at the wake, by lifting one the other by the legs, that one raised his comrade above the heads of the mourners that were watching, raised him so his face was to the window. And he roared out and his comrade dropped him, for he roared that Paudheen Ban a Cregan stood out there looking in, looking in on the window at his own wake. And then there was knocking on the door and no man had courage enough to open it, but when one did there stood the five Cregan men before him and spoke to him. But it was a long time before the people would believe they were alive. Now the first thing they told the company was how they were saved by that seal."

"It was a miracle," said the slow voice, and I was surprised to find that every man in the room, except me, knew exactly what had happened but was eager to hear it again. As it was the ferryman's turn to tell it, they waited after every interruption for him to go on in his own way.

"Well at that time there was a coastguard station near Killybegs in the County Donegal, fully sixty miles away to the north. And one morning early the watchman of the coastguard heard the roaring of a seal. 'Twas no way usual in that place and 'twas no usual way the seal was roaring either, but it did go on and on and on close about the shore, from one end to the other of the coastguard's place, until the watchman made sure there was something wrong, and he watching the seal swim up and down before him. He scanned the sea then with his telescope and saw nothing only this small craft far away against the sky. He took it to be the lifeboat maybe from some ship that was wrecked. So he called the others and they launched their galley and went out a long way till they came at the boat. And it wasn't a lifeboat at all. It was a curragh with an Irish-speaking crew— a crew of five Cregan men. But only one of them could speak, by the name of Paudheen Ban a Cregan, for the others had lost all power of sense and movement, and Paudheen Ban himself was weak as a sick old man. Well, they brought them ashore, but none could walk to the watchhouse only Paudheen Ban, so the coastguards cut sticks and tied bags on them for stretchers, and brought the others that way. 'Twas many days before they were strong enough to start for home and many more before they reached the country that they knew. They came on foot by the coasts of Donegal and Sligo and the coast of Mayo and at the end came into the village of Altmore the way I told you, on the night of their own wake. Now you will understand it was the seal that saved them, and to the people of Altmore, when once they did believe they saw before them five men and not five ghosts, it was like a resurrection. And so from that day to this there was never a seal killed by a man from Altmore."

"It were better," said the man in the corner, "for no man to kill a seal. Wasn't it your uncle, Michael, that killed the seal and died at the height of his strength?"

"He did. I am after telling this man how he was warned."

"What happened?" I said.

"Well, a lot of men those times liked to wear a waistcoat made of sealskin, and they made hats and caps out of sealskin too. There was nothing warmer against the wind and rain. This great-uncle of mine—Michael Sean—had a waistcoat like the rest, but he had it a long time and it was raggedy. The fur was wasted down the front of it, something like the skin of a mangy old cat. Its color was gray with black splashes on it, and it had a hole or two burned in it where he'd let his pipe fall with drink at the November Fair. Well, he was never married and the young women did annoy him putting shouts and laughter out of them when he walked the road. Oh they had him tormented with stories of how the holes came in his waistcoat. 'It's old like yourself,' they'd say to him. ' 'Tis the skin of an old seal that never had money nor land enough to get a wife. 'Tis the skin of that old seal that does be drinking rum at the November Fair.' "

When he heard Michael say this the man in the corner banged the floor with his stick and leant forward laughing. "That's right," he said loudly. "Oh yes, there was a seal drank rum at the November Fair."

"There was," said Michael. "And the women knew it. And so did he. But anyway he waits till the next fair day in Belmullet and he has a litter of young pigs to sell there. And he says to himself going over in the curragh, 'If I sell my pigs,' he says to himself, 'I'll take a glass or two with the man that buys them off me, and no more than that. I'll take one glass,' he says, and he rowing and thinking. 'Or if the company is good I'll maybe take three. But no more. I'll go home then early and I'll row myself home by myself and leave the fair. That way I'll be able to put in a couple of hours at the bog and bring home turf for the fire before night, and I'll have the money for the pigs in my pocket. For there's no sense,' he says to himself, when he's coming near to the pier of Belmullet, 'there's no sense at all in selling my pigs and spending half or more of the money in the public house after. And look at the grand drying day it is now,' he says to himself. 'It would surely be better for a man to come home and go to work in the evening, when the next day might be raining or he sick with the whisky.'

"Well, Michael Sean sold the pigs, but he was a long time selling them because he had that mood on him when a man is determined to hold out for his own price. And the price he got was a good price. 'Twas to a man by the name of Rory Mick he sold them. He knew the man well. They had many times sat together drinking and Rory Mick knew well that this great-uncle of mine was always the first to put his hand in his pocket and never the first to put down his glass and walk out. He was that way you see, more than some, for he was a great singer too and he was always kind of heedless and easy in his way when he came to the fair. At home he worked hard, but having no wife nor nothing he never gave much thought to the money while he was away. But this day he was quiet in himself because he was thinking how best to get away. And after the second glass he stood up.

" 'What's wrong?' says Rory Mick.

" 'There's nothing wrong at all, only my legs is stiff sitting.'

" 'Drink this,' says Rory Mick, 'and with the help of God 'twill loosen them.'

" 'Well, I will then and I thank you, but this is the third glass, and 'twill be the last if you'll excuse me.'

" 'I will excuse you surely,' says Rory Mick to my uncle, 'for there's no harm in a man standing to his drink. But I'm thinking,' says he, ' 'twill take ten and twenty glasses to loosen your tongue this day.'

" 'It's how I've no turf for the fire,' says my uncle then, 'and I'll need to get home before dark for to bring it in from the bog with the creel.'

" 'I'll tell you what I'll do,' says Rory. 'I have all my turf home in the rick days since and 'tis only a mile to my house beyond the town. We'll walk over presently there and I'll give you some in a bag. You can bring it with you in the boat then and 'twill do you till morning. But if I do,' says he, 'I suppose you will put your hand in your pocket once more and we'll have one glass more the two of us.'

"So they did, and if they had one they had twenty, and it was almost night when one in the company asks is there anything wrong with the lamp. Well, the lamp is burning rightly and there's no piece of the fire lying out on the floor, but there's a terrible smell of smoke, not a natural smell, like what you might notice when the jackdaws is nesting in the chimney, but a smell like the clippings of hair thrown on to a fire or the hoof of a horse when the smith puts the hot iron against it. And what is it, but my uncle's sealskin waistcoat, with the cinders of the pipe fallen down on it again and he lying back on the bench like one dead, but snoring.

"Well now, Rory Mick thought to spill a pint of porter on my uncle's waistcoat for to quench the fire, as he said to the company there, before he wakened. And this he did, for 'twould be a wicked thing, he told them, to let the poor old man waken and see his own waistcoat afire. It would frighten a man, and he in drink at the time. So Rory quenched the waistcoat with the porter. With the wetness of that on the skin of his chest, my great-uncle woke up, and when he looked at his waistcoat and saw they were laughing, he was like one suddenly mad. He thought they'd spoiled his waistcoat just to mock him, do you see? And he was an awful size of a man—big, big. So he picked up Rory Mick and he threw him into the crowd that was there, his head down on the head of another, and they not laughing more. And he took his ashplant, the same as that you have there, and he belted them. And when one that was behind him tore it from him, he took his two fists and belted them again till there wasn't a man of them standing, only two. And these two he picked up and he threw their heads against the wall of the hearth in such a way that one caught his coat alight with the fire. And the lamp fell to the floor. And every bench and stick in the place was smashed to pieces and began to burn. Now many said, after, how it was a marvel the thatch of the public house never went afire and how the people in it were not crushed and burned to death, and some of them lying stunned unconscious on the floor, and more of them drunk itself. But, it being Fair Day, the town was full and some went for buckets of water, and more beat the flames with twigs or what they could get hold of. When the fire was quenched they began to look for my great-uncle, but by this he was down to the pier and into his curragh and no one thought to search the sea.

"I don't know how he won home that night the way he was, but by good chance, the sea being calm and the moon clear, he made land on the long strand below his house across the water, a bit east of where we are sitting now. But instead of walking home he pulled the curragh up on the sand, and, being tired I suppose with the whisky and porter, he lay down beside it to sleep for himself. When he woke at the first light he did look at his waistcoat and saw it destroyed entirely with burns and porter and the marks of blood. Well, he was vexed and sick with the drink. He turned over on his side, I suppose, and he looked along the strand, and what did he see there but a young seal lying—a very young one it was, white, pure white and creamy, the color of a lamb.

" 'Now if I can get her,' he says to himself, 'I'll have the finest waistcoat in North Mayo. Indeed,' says he, 'I never saw a man with a white sealskin, for every waistcoat that I ever saw was made colory or gray from the skin of a seal that is grown. So if I can come at her,' says he to himself, 'I will kill that baby seal and skin her.'

"He took one of the oars and went down to the sea's edge. Crept along then, crept along till he came between her and the water; though, if she was as white in her coat as they say, I suppose it was doubtful had she learned to swim. But anyway he came there and he rushed her, hit her five or six belts of the oar and laid her dead. And if he did, there was a terrible wailing in the sea."

"It was the mother," said the man in the corner.

"Michael Sean was afraid in his heart, but he put the baby into his creel and slung her on his back and walked home. He did not want the neighbors to know of his new waistcoat until he had made it, so he took her beyond the gable end of his house where no one might see him from the road. He skinned her then. He saved the fat. There's a terrible lot of fat on a young seal and he put that away somewhere and began to stretch the skin and to cure it. Then he looked up from his work and he saw a woman standing near him. 'Good day,' says he to her, but she never said 'God bless the work' nor nothing.

" 'I have seen you before,' says he to her again.

" 'You have, and I often thanked God for your kindness,' says she. 'For it is many's the time you gave me potatoes and buttermilk and a place for myself by the fire in years gone by—a poor old traveling woman like myself, God bless you.'

" 'Indeed I disremembered it for a minute,' says Michael Sean. 'But now I know you well.'

" 'That's a very young seal you have there.'

" 'It is. It is.'

" 'Did you strike and kill that seal?'

" 'I did—yes,' says Michael Sean. 'I struck her with the oar of my curragh on the strand below.'

" 'I am afraid,' she says, looking at him, 'there is harm in that for you.'

" 'Indeed,' says Michael Sean, 'I never heard there was anything wrong in killing a seal for her skin.'

" 'And what happened to your face that's all blood and scars?' she says.

" 'I slipped on the rock below,' says he, for he didn't want her to know what had happened at the Fair.

"He gave her food and a silver piece that he had still from the pigs and nothing more was said about the seal until she turned from his door to travel on. He was afraid then by what she said first and he asked her again what harm he had done. And she said, 'It is my sharp sorrow that I tell you, but there is harm for you within a year on account of what you did to that young seal. And,' she says, 'I am frightened for you too when I know it was you set the public house alight in Belmullet.'

" 'Does the police know it was me?' he says.

" 'No one will tell the police,' says she. 'They are afraid for themselves.'

" 'But someone has told you,' says he to her, and when she told him no, that she'd seen no one and hadn't been anywhere near to Belmullet on the day of the Fair, he began to be sore afraid there was truth in what she said about the seal.

"Anyway, she went from him and he had the grand new waistcoat made, and when it came round again to next November Fair, didn't he wear it to Belmullet, and didn't the people remark on it, every one, and ask him had he found a chest of gold washed up from some old ship, or was he marrying the landlord's daughter, or the queen herself, that after all his life of wearing the one sealskin waistcoat, he was dressed so fine at last. Well, the next day, which was one year after the killing of the baby seal, he went to work on the bog, just

where I was working today, the very same place. And he was found
the next morning on the bank dead with his hat tumbled down on
the road. He was found, as I told this man today, by that same traveling woman who had warned him. That's all I know about it."

The landlord came in with a paraffin lamp, which he hung on the
wall, and now I could see the three other men as they sat with black
pints in their hands. The one opposite me was about eighteen. He
had not spoken. He sat very still and looked straight ahead of him,
his face in perfect repose, his limbs and body relaxed. I thought that
wherever he went there would go with him a feeling of grace and
ease. The man in the corner was lively and excitable, old, with round
shoulders, a narrow body, a face full of sudden movement, wide in
the mouth, with large brown eyes and puffy cheeks that gave him
sometimes the look of a woman, aged and knowing. When the others
said anything that touched his memories he would bang the floor
with his ashplant.

"Tell us now," he said to Michael the Ferry, "of the seal that went
to the Fair of Belmullet and drank rum."

"I don't know is that story true."

" 'Tis true enough."

"Well now, there's some of the same family alive today, and they
not far from here."

"That's true," said the man in the corner, hitting the floor again.

"And I think," said Michael the Ferry, "it mightn't be right to tell
the story in a public place."

"Well. Well."

"There was nothing in that story that a person would be inclined
to take exception to," said the man with the slow voice. "Except
maybe those individuals whose ancestors it does come on."

"It's them that denies it," said the man in the corner.

And Michael the Ferry put an end to this by saying, "I think if it
was about my own and the people laughing at me for it, I might
deny it too."

The man with the slow voice was separated from the others by
the way he spoke and by his manner. He had the steadiness and ease

of the young man opposite to me, but there was something author-itative in his quiet gestures that made one glance at him and wait for him to speak. When he spoke in English it was with the same accent as the others, but his words and phrases were chosen with care. I was not at all surprised when he told me later that he had spent twenty years in the British army, and that he had read a large num-ber of English books since he learned the language at school.

"What you tell me of your ancestor," he now said to Michael the Ferry, politely helping to suppress the other story, "was quite a com-mon occurrence in days gone by."

"I believe there was some had warning from the seals them-selves," said the man in the corner.

"There was Boyle," said the man with the slow voice.

"Had he warning of a seal?"

"It was of a traveling woman just the same as Michael Sean."

Everybody waited as he drew the palm of his hand over his mouth, collecting himself as though to make a set speech.

"It was sixty or seventy years ago," he said, and waited again. "Yes, seventy years ago there lived in Carrickbeg a man whose name was Boyle. He was a great fisherman, but one day he came home with a seal, a colored seal with spots on it, a very nice seal; he brought it home specially for the purpose of getting the skin of it, you know, for making a garment out of it, or selling it rather. He brought it home in a creel from Altmore, and when he came home he took the seal out of the creel and he left it down at the end of the house, at the end of the kitchen of the house. Shortly afterward it happened that a beggar woman came along, a traveling woman—they were very numerous in those days—and she came in to the house and she saw the seal. She examined it. 'Oh,' she said, 'you have done a very wrong thing to kill and take home that seal. Before this day three months you'll have reason to regret your action.' Well, she went away and they took no more notice of her tongue. But it wasn't three months from that day until that man and his two sons were drowned in the Bay of Broad Haven as they were going in their curragh for sea-wrack. Were you ever in a curragh?" he said at the end to me.

"It was in the big wooden boat we came across," said Michael the Ferry.

I suddenly remembered the boy. "What about the boy?"

"Oh, he'll play for himself on the strand another while yet."

It was dark and we could hear the rain on the window.

"I have been in a curragh," I said.

"It's a coracle you call them in England, I believe."

"Yes—but the boat they call a coracle is almost round. It is made the same way, but there's no real bow or stern to it. It's like a big saucer about three feet across."

"Is that so?"

"Yes. You don't have oars, you have one paddle. I've even seen a man lie flat on his belly and row his coracle along with his hands, as though he was swimming."

" 'Twould go hard with him in a heavy sea," said Michael.

"It was on a river the one I saw—on the River Severn."

"And how many men will it carry?"

"I'm not sure. There was only me and the man who owned it in the one I saw, and we seemed well down in the water. But he told me he could carry two or three hundredweight of stuff."

"He could, I'm sure, if he had it rightly built. Was it out of hide he had it built?"

"No. Calico. Tarred, just like your curragh."

"Well, in times gone by," said the man with the slow voice, "they made the curraghs out of cowhide, stretched over a wooden frame."

"They would be heavier, I'm thinking," said Michael the Ferry.

"They must have been altogether heavier, because I don't suppose they had the same light laths that we get. Well, if you have been in a curragh you'll know there is only this thin piece of calico between you and eternity. That's all."

"I do believe," said Michael the Ferry, "that that English kind of a curragh would bring him nearer to eternity than you or I have been, no matter what storms we were at sea in."

"Like a saucer, did you say?" said the man in the corner, waving his ashplant in a circle. "Well now, I wouldn't like to go to sea in one of those machines."

By this time, although it was ten o'clock at night, the front part of the shop was crowded with men and women buying and talking and looking at newspapers. Michael the Ferry went out among them, the young man moved in his leisurely way and leant against the partition, and the other two stood up as if to go but remained by the barrels talking about cattle. I thought this meant that Michael was on his way to get the boat ready, so after I had finished my drink I went out to look for him, to thank him and to say good night. He was sitting on a pile of nets by the door of the shop.

"Will I ask herself to make your bed here?" he said.

"You could introduce me to her. I wasn't sure who to ask."

"She'll be with you now."

People greeted him by the door as they came in and out, and spoke to him about the death of his wife. A woman in a black shawl gave him a parcel and a long verbal message to deliver, and the postman handed him a bundle of newspapers.

Some time later he said, "She has two rooms above."

"D'you think one of them is empty?"

"Oh surely. There's no strangers here today, only yourself. At this time of the year there's very few traveling, only the dentist on his two days and the vet an odd night."

"Will you be over here again tomorrow?"

"I will of course. I'm to bring the police over in the morning."

"You'll call in here?"

"I will surely. I'll bring you back with me if you wish. I've to wait till such time as the police have their business finished and then I'll bring you with them. It is usually in this house I wait."

"I'd like to hear more about these seals."

He laughed. "I think you heard this night all there is to hear."

"Perhaps. Is that the woman of the house behind the counter now?"

"It is. That's herself. A fine strong woman isn't she?"

"I'll go and ask her now."

"If you wish."

"I'll be back."

"If you wish to stay with me in the ferry house across, you are welcome."

"Wouldn't that be a trouble?"

"Not at all. You are welcome."

"It's very kind of you."

"This house is a good house, and there's no better people than that woman you see there and himself. But here you would be with strangers and there is little comfort in that."

"I'll come with you, then. Thank you."

We waited another half-hour or so, and when we did at last leave there was no way of telling what moved him. He just nodded a "good night" and walked out.

I followed. It seemed to me that we had left the others behind, but as we turned at the end of the pathway on to the sandy beach I saw they had reached the boat before us. We pushed the boat into the water. Mickeen and I climbed into the stern and we rowed across to the ferry house. Nobody spoke on the way over.

THE FERRY HOUSE WAS BUILT CLOSE TO THE WATER, of rough stone loosely mortared. It had three rooms, two small bedrooms at the gable ends and a long kitchen in the center. It was thatched with rushes that gave to its roof a thinner look than any thatch seen in England. The walls were whitewashed, streaked green and muddy near the ground by the rain and the spray from the sea. The door facing the sea was in two parts—a half-door as they call it. The upper half was opened as we came near and a strip of yellow light fell rippling on the sea. A second door, at the back of the kitchen, for use when the wind blew from the sea, was usually kept closed. It was opposite to us as we went in. Michael the Ferry led the way and we found seats for ourselves on benches and wooden chairs. The kitchen was like the seal-killer's kitchen, but without the loft, and almost everything in it had to do with work. The rafters were hung with brown nets in uneven loops, some of them slung lengthways on old oars; the pegs on the back of the far door held pieces of an ass's harness. There were basket creels, lobster pots, a spade, a double-barreled gun, a tall dash churn for butter, buoys and hurricane lamps and several pairs of oars, all casting shadows on the walls and floor in untraceable shapes.

In the darkest corner, hidden by the shadows, I saw something like a low wooden chest, black, with an open top. It seemed to be filled with sacks or blankets, and I was startled when I glanced again to see the head of a child looking over the side, then another, then a third, gazing with wide and bright eyes at me, the stranger, but sinking down silently out of sight whenever they caught my eye. After he had had a cup of tea and eaten bread and butter with us, Mickeen was taken by the woman who now looked after the house, undressed and put to bed with the others. She moved about in bare feet silently and never spoke except to greet us when we first arrived, or in whispers now and then to the children. She was not yet thirty, lean and handsome, but all softness had been taken from her by weather and hard work. After she had put Mickeen to bed she left the house carrying with her the baby in a shawl.

"Don't forget now to rake the fire," she said to Michael from the door.

"Good night," said Michael, and when she had gone he said, "I did forget it one night and we had no kindling and all was wet with the rain outside, so she has never forgiven me the hour she had trying to light it next day, and the sods cold and wet in her hand, the creature. She's a fine woman, God bless her. Only for her I doubt would the baby be alive this day."

"Has she far to go now?" I said.

"About a mile. She'll bring that baby everywhere with her just as she would her own. She'll bring him home now and back here again in the morning when she comes to see after the others. And there's no loss on him. He is stronger every day, God bless him."

It must have been almost midnight by now, but the company had not changed; Patrick Sean Cregan—the man in the corner—now in another corner by the fire; Joseph Tom Cregan, the young man, beside him, leaning back against the wall; the man with the slow voice on a chair, with one arm resting on the table, and Michael the Ferry in his own place by the fire. I was surprised and glad when they did not leave us at the quay and now hoped it would not bore them to turn the conversation back to seals. A long silence came and I had forgotten about the baby when the man with the slow voice said:

"There's no loss on a child with a foster mother, Michael, no loss at all."

Michael nodded beside the fire and Patrick Sean from his corner shouted:

"Look at Patsy Colehan, him with the long arms. He's one. He's one. I've seen him carry fifteen ewes across the big bank when the flood was on. In a couple of hours he had them safe, himself alone."

"That is true, Patrick Sean, and the brothers born previously to him were useless."

"But with them," said Michael the Ferry, "it was how their mother was sick all her life."

"She was," said the man in the corner. "And she had no sense neither."

"But my woman," said Michael, "was a good woman, God have mercy on her, and she had never a day's sickness all her life."

"It was the will of God, Michael, and she made a beautiful corpse."

"She went out with the ebb tide," said Michael the Ferry, "the way I knew she would, for I was looking from the window when God took her and I never saw the water lower than it was that minute. I thought to myself, and I still praying, if God spares her now for these few minutes, and the tide to turn, she will be safe."

"It was the will of God," said the man with the slow voice.

"Do you remember the small little cow?" said Patrick Sean from his corner.

"The Kerry cow, is it?" said Michael.

"No, no. The small little cow."

"The Jersey cow," said the man with the slow voice. "Of course I remember her well."

"Ye had no right to buy her," said Michael, "and I told ye that the day ye drove her home."

"Well now, she was a good cow."

"She was a good cow at home with her own people, maybe, but all the grass in County Mayo wouldn't feed her, little and all as she was."

"Well now, she was a good price. She wasn't dear." Each time, before he answered, he drew himself in and paused.

"She wasn't cheap then and she to die within the year."

"Those species of cows," said the man with the slow voice, "are accustomed to be housed in the winter time."

"In England they do put every cow into a house," said Michael, looking at me for confirmation.

"Well now," said the man in the corner, "it wasn't the grass of Mayo, nor the hard weather that killed her. It was them that put her to the wrong class of a bull."

"Was she in calf when you bought her?"

"She was of course. And that's how they had me blackguarded, for no man could tell me rightly where this little cow was from, and when I did ask what bull had covered her they told me 'twas one of her own kind."

"And where would you find a Jersey bull in Ireland?" said Michael the Ferry. "Did ye never think of that when you were bidding for her?"

"You might see a Jersey bull in the County Meath," said the man with the slow voice. "And in County Dublin you'll see them. They are wicked I believe."

"Well now," said the man in the corner, "you saw this small little cow yourself and she was kind. There was never a kinder one to milk. You'd know that by her head."

"She was then, quiet and generous. I did often remark it, Patrick Sean."

"I had feeling for her when I saw her on the street, and there was a big crowd about her, for no man had seen one like her, but no man would bid for her, she being strange to the country, which is how I had her at so small a price."

"It was of course," said Michael the Ferry.

Patrick Sean began to wave his ashplant in the air again.

"She gave the best of milk all summer," he said quietly. Then he shouted, "But when she came to calve 'twas then I saw how them devils had me robbed. I did have to cut the calf from her. Did ye remember that?"

"Sure, weren't we all with ye," said Michael the Ferry, "where she'd wandered down by the shore, and she calving."

"The tide was well down at the time," said Patrick Sean, speaking quietly again. "Do you think, Michael, supposing I to have waited till the tide was full again, would she have calved rightly for herself then?"

"You often asked me that, but I think she would have died no matter what we did. With that size of a calf any small cow would die. But if she chose to die at the ebb o' the tide, then no matter had we waited or not she would die later, for the tide would ebb again."

I asked whether death always came at low tide and Michael answered. "No. But if a beast or person is anyways weak, then their strength will fail and build with the ebb and flow. 'Tis just the same as with the moon, though you wouldn't remark it in yourself, your mind being strong; if you watch a person that's weak in the mind you will see how his sense comes and goes with the moon."

Mickeen's voice came from the box-bed and the three heads looked out with his.

"Did Brigid Ann Moloney go out of her mind with the moon?"

"She did not, Mickeen. She was born with that weakness, God bless her."

"She gave me a skylark's egg."

"She's a kind-hearted girl, the poor soul."

"She's a good one to find a nest, isn't she, Da?"

"She is. Go to sleep now, the crowd o' ye."

"Brigid Ann promised to give me a hawk's egg next summer."

"Lie down and go asleep now, will ye."

The heads went down again but there was whispering and some laughter in the bed.

"This man," said Michael the Ferry a few minutes later, "has a great thought for the seals."

"Would you like to go shooting them?" said the man with the slow voice.

"No, but I was telling Michael before we left that I'd like to hear some more about them."

"I'm much afraid you heard all," said Michael again.

Everyone was quiet until the young man spoke. It was the first time he had spoken that evening.

"Do you remember the seal we met outside the chapel? That was a very young seal, Michael, that one. 'Twas a kind of yellow-white one. I saw it."

"I think 'twas wrong to kill it."

"It was how Pat Finney thought it would spoil his hay. There was a shocking smell off this one." He laughed and then said, " 'Twas Pat Finney killed it in the end. You remember how 'twas walking on the road outside the chapel, like any dog, and when the people came out for Mass didn't it follow them—'twas like a tame seal. It followed the two Finney girls, and they only going to school at the time, the same age as myself, and Finoola, she was one to do any mad thing and she took the reins off of my ass cart, and I driving my mother home from Mass without the reins after, and she tied them to the neck of this young seal. And led the creature after her, she and her sister letting screams out of them all the way from Mass."

"It is easy to tame them when they are young."

"Well now, that's what Finoola was at. She had it dragged into the haggard and the fence closed on it; she thought to leave it there and feed fish to it. But when Pat Finney, the father, went to the rick that evening to pull out a lock of hay for his two beasts, didn't he smell her there, and he said she had the hay destroyed on him. No beast would touch it. They'd starve on him before the springtime! Oh, roaring and shouting! You know the way he is. If he was only asking the loan of a spade you'd hear him the other side of the ferry. Oh, dear God . . . "

"Well?" said the man in the corner when the boy couldn't go on for laughing.

"Well anyway he went for his gun and he shot the seal where it lay shut in the haggard. That's how it was."

"It were better for him to have nothing to do with it," said the man in the corner, "or to let it loose and find its own road down to the sea."

"Well nothing went wrong after. He's strong yet, old Pat, and still roaring. But the mother seal came up from the sea that evening and she was all night keening and crying round about the house. 'Twas a terrible sound to hear."

"I have heard it," said the man in the corner, "and I have heard a young one crying just like any Christian baby, and its mother lying dead on a table in the room where we were at the seal-killer's house. The young one would go up to drink at her breast and she dead, and as he would drink a little, he was crying for his mother. He was crying over her, and after he'd drink a few sups more, he'd cry again."

"There's no better mother than the seal," said the man with the slow voice.

"A seal's breast milk will raise an inch of fat. Isn't that what it says in the proverb?" said Michael.

I asked whether people used to drink it, but no one had heard of that.

"They must," said Michael, "when they made the proverb that way."

"They might have been referring to the nourishment the young seal has," said the man with the slow voice.

"They might, they might well, for there's no other creature as fat."

"And the oil from the fat was a great benefit to the people along this coast. It was a panacea for numerous ills, as you know, especially for rheumatism and all that kind of thing. And I know, too, that the milk of a seal was beneficial."

"For people?" I said.

"For babies."

"Human babies?"

"For seals and human babies."

"How was it used? I mean how would you get it?"

"Well now, the seal and mermaid are both mammalians, you must understand. They both suckle their young from the breast."

"Yes."

"Well then, I'll tell you a story about what happened in that connection a long long time ago now in a village on the northern coast of Erris. It was the practice of the fisherfolk of that place to be killing and catching seals for their skins and for making seal oil, as you have heard. But on this particular day there was a man there in this seaside village and he thought the day and the occasion was favorable to go seal-hunting. He went to a neighbor's house and he called on his neighbor to go along with him out to the seal caves. And it so happened that this man that he called on had his wife absent from home, and there was a little baby in the cradle, and the man of the house said to this man that called on him, 'Well I'm sorry,' he said, 'I cannot go with you, there's a little baby in the cradle and there's no one to look after it in my absence; my wife has gone from home.'

" 'That's too bad, it's a good day for the purpose of catching a seal, I don't know what we'll do. But I'll tell you,' he said, 'what's the best thing we can do—take the little baby with you. We'll take him out in the curragh with us to the seal caves. The day's fine and he'll be quite comfortable in the curragh. He'll be just as well off,' he says, 'as lying there in his cradle.'

" 'A very good thought, I'll take him.'

"He wrapped him up in a piece of blanket, a shawl, or some sort of swaddling clothes, put the little bundle under his arm and went down to the beach, put out the curragh, placed the little bundle in the bow of the curragh and set out quite happily for the seal caves; went along, came to the mouth of the cave. For greater safety the father took the little infant, the little baby, took him out of the curragh and went in the cave and placed him up on a little shelf or ledge in the side of the cave and left him there. Then they proceeded inward and suddenly a mighty wave arose, what they call a ground swell suddenly arose and it started to bombard them out of the cave. So fearing that their exit was cut off they rushed, the two men, rushed for the curragh, which was lying at the mouth of the cave, moored there, and they got into the curragh just in time—they just narrowly escaped being engulfed in the mighty billow thundering at the mouth of the cave.

"In their precipitancy and excitement they forgot all about the little baby which was left on the shelf of the cave. They couldn't get back to rescue it; they'd get lost; and there was nothing they could do but to turn home without it. They came sorrowfully home, landed home, having lost what they thought was the baby. The neighbors dropped into the house that night, to wake the baby in the traditional way for that night and the succeeding night.

"Well, in a day or two afterward, in about two days after, or say about on the third day, the storm at sea subsided and the sea became calm, and the man said, 'Well,' to his neighbor, 'well, we'll go out again and see if we can find any trace of the little baby, of its body; there's no chance that he'll be living.'

"Out they went, returned again to the mouth of the cave. It was quite calm and as they were going into the cave they saw a big, huge, old seal, an old mother seal, nursing what they thought was a baby seal, nursing it at the breast in the manner of human beings or of a human mother. And as they were approaching this old seal, she dropped this object that she was nursing at the breast, dropped it on the ground on the floor of the cave and rushed for the water—she wasn't far from the water, of course—and disappeared into the sea. But she left this little object behind. They went up and examined it, thinking that they were going to find a baby seal, but instead they found their own baby, the baby that they had abandoned the first day through stress of storm.

"They took the baby. He was quite warm, quite warm and quite comfortable, and took him away with them very gladly and put him into the curragh and made for home as fast as possible; brought him home to the great rejoicing of the neighbors who all flocked in to congratulate the baby and the people on the recovery of the lost infant. And he grew up to be a great man, a fine young man, and a remarkable swimmer. He was a great swimmer."

"Yes. Yes, that's true," said the man in the corner. "I heard my mother tell it."

"How long ago do you think it was?" I asked them.

The man in the corner did not know, and the man with the slow voice said, "It certainly didn't happen since the French landing in Killala. That would be a hundred and fifty years ago. It was before that, possibly not very long before that."

When he heard this, Mickeen put his head up over the edge of the box-bed and asked for a rhyme about what the seal says.

"Lie down and go asleep," said his father. "He has me tormented for these rhymes."

"There is no rhyme for the seal," the old man said.

"But the seals can speak and cry better than the sea gulls," said Mickeen. "They do sound more like a person when they cry."

"They do indeed."

"Well then, they should be able to say something for themselves in a rhyme."

"Indeed I think they lost the power of speech long ago." The old man tapped the bed with his ashplant.

"Then they did speak one time?"

"Go asleep, will ye," said Michael the Ferry, but the old man would not help him.

"They say all the animals and birds had the power of speech long ago."

"A hundred and fifty years ago?" said Mickeen, putting his head out again. "That's long enough ago for them to speak surely. That's long enough ago for them to say a rhyme."

"It is, I think. I think they had the power of speech in my father's father's day."

"Then what did they say?"

"God bless ye, child, I don't know what they'd say."

The man with the slow voice spoke then: "I often heard the seals will mourn their own dead."

"They will," said Michael the Ferry. "And they'll mourn a dead Christian too."

"Did you ever hear them at it?"

"I did," the old man said.

"I never did myself," said Michael the Ferry, "but I heard tell of it, and 'twas my father said it when he told me of his father's funeral."

"Many a man was afraid when he heard it," the old man said. "And he after killing the seals himself."

"That's true," said the man with the slow voice. "There was a crew out, a fishing crew, fishing and killing seals at the same time, and they went into a cave and they attacked and killed a number of seals in the cave. They took them away with them, the dead bodies of the seals, and they hadn't gone out very far until all the seals, of which there was a terrible number, started roaring and bawling, and they set up a terrible hullabaloo about the dead seals. And amidst all the excitement and turmoil one seal was heard to exclaim: 'Who killed Anna? Who killed Anna? Who killed Anna?' And this was answered by another seal: 'Oh, the same man, the man always, the man always, the man always.' That is, 'the same man, the same man, the same man.'"

As he spoke the words of the seal he leant back on the bench and howled. Mickeen was pleased and I saw him staring and hoping for more. The old man helped.

"There was a man called Diarmid ac Eoghain," he said, "and he got great sport out of shooting seals. It wasn't so long ago. Oh, he used to be out every day with his gun shooting them as fast as he met them, until one day he saw a mother seal and a young one along with her. But didn't she speak when he raised his gun! 'Don't, don't, Diarmid ac Eoghain,' said she, 'till I give the breast to my little one.' 'I won't or ever again,' said Diarmid to her. And they say he never shot a seal from that day on."

"Go asleep, will ye, Mickeen," said Michael the Ferry, but at that moment the old man brought his ashplant down again on the side of the boy's bed. "And I heard a woman say," he shouted louder than before, "and it was my mother said it, that there were two men east of Altmore and their trade was killing seals, and they used long spears with iron tips for to kill them. Well, this day they were east at Leacht Murcha, down low on the cliff with their spears. And 'twas an awkward place to keep a foothold, with the slope and slipperiness of the rock. One o' these men made a drive at a seal below him with his spear, but the spear hit the rock and slid aside, and with losing his balance he was thrown down the slope. And he was hurted. ' 'Tis a pity,' said he, 'that I didn't stay at home today.' ' 'Tis a pity you didn't,' said the seal back to him. He was sore afraid with that."

"Was that the usual way of killing seals round here?" I asked him.

"This spear was one way, but some would shoot them, and more would attack them with clubs. There was one man living here by the name of Michael Martin that dug holes in the sand and covered them with sticks and seaweed. He caught them that way, for when they went to cross the sticks their great weight would bring them into the hole."

The man with the slow voice laughed. "There's a proverb out of that," he said.

"There is. Well, 'twas Michael Martin made the proverb the day he put no traps. He went down to the strand this day and he saw plenty of seals, and they sporting and playing with one another—enjoying themselves the way you'll often see them—and no traps to stop them. So he calls out to them. 'Ye may be thankful,' he shouts to them, and they playing."

"Did they answer?" said Mickeen, with his head up again.

"They did not," said Patrick Sean.

"Go asleep, will ye," said Michael, sounding more calm and ineffectual every time he said it.

"But out of that," said Patrick Sean, turning to me, "we have the proverb, 'Be thankful, as Michael Martin said to the seals.' You can say that to one who has escaped some wrong, and he not knowing it."

The thought of this proverb made everyone laugh. Even the impassive face of the young man broke into laughter, while Patrick Sean himself lost all control, dropped his ashplant on the floor, covered his face with his hands and leant forward shaking. But suddenly he looked seriously at me and said:

"The seals spoke no word to him, you understand, but it were better for him to find some other trade."

"Did he?"

"No. I never heard that Michael Martin was a bit afraid—and no harm came to him, or if it did he kept it to himself. But if it was myself that made the proverb, I'd be afraid lest it would turn against myself."

"You mean," said Michael the Ferry, "the seals might say to you 'be thankful' and you not know why they said it."

"That's what I mean."

"But I thought you said you never killed a seal," I said.

"I never did. 'Tis a thing I would not do if I could help it, but I oftentimes did catch them in the trammels o' the nets and once I found one drownded in the nets."

"That did you no harm, sure," said Michael the Ferry.

"Amn't I after telling you how I lost the small little cow? And where did she choose to calve, only on the strand where Michael Martin hunted them? 'Twas there I had my boat the day I caught the dead one."

"That was years before," the young man said.

"It was but it makes no differ."

"You could say the same of everything that happened to you, Patrick Sean. You can blame last year's harvest on to that seal. There was more than one cow died on you in years gone by. I'm sure of that."

"There was. And I've had fine, strong beasts die on me with the black leg—and I've lost sheep with the flood. But you are young. You know nothing."

"Indeed I'm not saying I'm right, Patrick Sean. But wasn't it yourself said the little cow was put to the wrong class of a bull?"

"She was. They had me robbed, bad cess to them. But it would be better for you to take notice of an old man like myself—because there's many things may happen in your life too, and the reason for them hard to come at."

I said, "So you think it was the seal you found dead that brought bad luck?"

"I was afraid when I saw her dead. I put her down in the water as soon as I had her free o' the net, but it wasn't three days before she was washed up on this same shore below my house."

"Did the other seals cry for her?" said Michael the Ferry.

"They did not. But I'll tell you what put fear on me, Michael. It was something I heard told and I heard there's no word of a lie in it either. And it happened close by where we are sitting. There were two men left the quay, by the door here, and they were fishing mackerel out by night in the bay beyond, and when they hauled their net there was a young seal among the fish in the net, just the same way I suppose as I did catch my seal. But this seal the two men caught was alive. No loss on him at all. Well, they took him, one of them took him, and when he got him home he turned him out and put him under a basket, put him under it."

Patrick Sean was excited by his dispute with the young man. He started coughing. He repeated phrases, banging the children's bed with his ashplant for emphasis. He coughed violently, spat into the fire, and croaked on.

"They put him under the basket. I don't know whether they gave him any fish to eat or not or what they did do. But they went out again the next night and the most lonely noise they ever heard was near the boat. "Have you seen Donagh? Have you seen Donagh?" And the wailing went on the whole night, lonely on the sea, and it black with darkness. And the men came in before it was day at all and when they came to the house, they came into the house and they were telling the people that were inside that whatever was wrong, or whatever was going to happen, it was the most lonely noise they ever heard, and it was all around the boat all night—and it wailing, "Have you seen Donagh?" They came inside in the house and told the people that, told them that."

Confused and hurried, he stopped and said no more, but because he plainly believed and feared this memory more than what had gone before, he made us fear it too. After another long silence the young man said without skepticism, "And what came out of it, Patrick Sean?"

"I never heard."

"Did they let the young seal go?" said Michael the Ferry.

"I never heard what happened after."

"Well I believe if they put him out they'd be all right," said Michael, "because I know my father, when he was a young lad, did the same. He brought home a young seal and put him down in the kitchen here for the night, and in the night there was a voice outside the door and it crying, 'Tadhg has left me!' and this seal in the corner of the kitchen here let words out of him when he heard the crying. 'I am Tadhg,' says this seal. When my father's father heard that he said to my father, who was only young at the time and had little understanding: 'Go,' he said, 'and take that seal and put him out the door by the water's edge and leave him there. Say nothing,' he said to my father; 'only go and leave him there by the water.' And when my father opened out the door, there he saw another seal on the quay waiting. If there's harm in the seal, Patrick Sean, there is good in him, only that a man who is fishing and working near to where those creatures have their living, then he must study their ways."

"They have been of great benefit to all classes of people," said the man with the slow voice.

"It is better to have nothing to do with them," said Patrick Sean, "no matter is it good nor bad."

"I don't know are you right," said Michael the Ferry. "Do you remember how Mrs. McKinley lost her child?"

"I do," said Patrick Sean. "Wasn't it into the sea the child fell?"

"Not at all. 'Twas in a place down the cliff. It was how the McKinley man's cattle came off o' the mountain one day and went galloping through the tillage lands. That's how it happened."

"Was it mad with the warble-fly they were?" the old man said.

"I suppose."

"There's nothing in the world worse with cattle."

"Did you ever try the new dressing?" the young man said.

"I tried motor oil and sulfur powder mixed. I smeared their backs with it, every one. But it was useless."

"Well, this stuff now that they're selling in Belmullet is good, but I disremember the name. It's very good, only that you have to dress them with it every couple of days."

"Now that's little use to a man if he must do that," said Michael the Ferry, "and his cattle above on the mountain, a full day's walk to come at them, and then home again at night."

"That's true."

"Well," said Patrick Sean, "was it how the McKinley cattle frightened the young child?"

"Not at all. But 'twas a hot summer's day when my mother was a little girl. 'Twas she told me this herself for she was there. And this family McKinley was living next door to my mother's house in the village of Altmore. On that day there was no one at home in the McKinley's house, only the woman of the house and a little boy of hers, about three or four years old. The man o' the house was away line fishing that day, for mackerel, with some others of a crew, and the weather being good there was no man at home in the village. So there was no way for her, only to go herself to drive her cattle off o' the neighbor's crops. They were stopped by the wall beyond, you understand, and when she came to them they were eating the green corn, grazing a piece and running on another piece, the way they are when they're uneasy in themselves."

"Yes, yes," said Patrick Sean. "They are devils when they hear the fly."

"Well they had plenty of damage done and a terrible bawling and shouting out of them when she made to go to them. But to bring the little gossoon with her was a thing she could not do. She could not carry him and drive the cattle, and I suppose if she let him follow her she'd be afraid he might be hurted by those beasts. So she put him in a garden of potatoes that was behind the house, himself and the little dog with him, and she told him to play there for himself with the dog and not move from that place until she'd be back. Well, she gathered the beasts and put them into a piece of grassland that was fenced with a wall away from the crops. She didn't trouble to put them back on the mountain, because she was thinking of the little gossoon. But quick and all as she was, she had to close a gap in the wall, and when she came into the garden of potatoes, the little boy was gone."

"She was distressed, I'm sure," said the man with the slow voice.

"She made then a desperate search. She went to every house to see would she get word of him. But no one had seen him. No trace of him, nor the dog, no word of them. She remembered then how the child's father used to bring him with him sometimes to the strand, to the boat, and it put the heart across her to think of it, so she ran down to the sea, and there sure enough her heart was nearly broken, for, in a soft patch of sand beside the water's edge, there she saw the footprints of her child."

"He was drowned," said the man with the slow voice.

"She made sure to herself he was drowned. And every woman of the village of Altmore was searching the shore for that little gossoon. And she herself left them there. She was distracted. She went along by the cliff tops then, above, and she running, and she crying and wailing for the child. But very soon she heard another crying like herself, and 'twas a woman, and she stood still to listen, but she couldn't tell from where it came, and she ran to and hither, and she stood still again, and she listening for this cry. So she went to where she thought she heard the voice. On then she ran to a place where the cliff dipped down in a kind of a cleft, and there she thought the voice was stronger. And there what did she see when she climbed down but a great seal standing up in the sea a little way off from the shore and crying out and wailing like a woman. So she climbed down further, down this cleft o' the cliff, and there by a piece of rock that stood between her and the water, she did hear the crying of a child. And the crying of the seal was in her ears too. So down further she traveled among the rocks, and there she did find her boy, himself and the dog that was with him."

"I am sure she was thankful," said the man with the slow voice.

"She was of course. Herself and the McKinley man when he came home from the fishing that night—they knew well the child was lost only for that seal. He would never, being only a little gossoon, be able to climb back up the cliff, d'ye see, and his cries were lost in that lonely place. So she brought him home and she was glad. And by this the McKinley man was home too."

"He would be thankful," said the man with the slow voice.

"He was indeed. He heard every kind of story when he came from the shore about how the child was drowned in the sea. But he was thankful when he saw the gossoon. So whenever the father came back from the fishing after that day, he would bring a lock of fish to that cleft o' the cliff and put it on a rock for the seal. And the seal would swim in close when he saw the McKinley man come near. The seal would eat the fish and swim away. She was well known, that seal."

I said, "How was she known?"

"She was known by everyone in that place. She was oftentimes about. And the McKinley man put fish for her on to this rock for years. Until, at the end, she came no more. She would have died, or maybe she was killed. There is no way to know. But it was many years that the McKinley man was feeding her."

The man with the slow voice said, "They are noted for their longevity, the seals," and I asked what age they would live to.

"There is no way to know."

"The one we saw today was an old one," said Michael the Ferry. "I think you can tell by the size of him, and he was big."

"That's right," said the young man. "It does be the very same with fish. The mackerel, now, he'll grow until the day he dies."

"He will," said Patrick Sean, "and the salmon the same."

"The seal we saw today," said Michael the Ferry, "was apt to win against the run of the tide. He was strong, but the tide had him beat."

"Was he the size of a government boar?" the young man asked.

"He was, and more."

"Any seal is the size of that," said Patrick Sean, "and more."

"I don't know then. We had a boar on the scales and he weighed three hundred."

"He'd be a Large White, was he?"

"He was."

"Well I never had a seal on the scales, so I don't know what's in that. But a good-sized bull seal is larger than a boar, and softer. He's a good weight." Patrick Sean laid his ashplant on the floor as he said this. "And if he's a good weight, he'll chase and kill big mackerel."

"Is the seal faster than the mackerel?" I said.

"She is of course. Unless the King Mackerel has her beat."

Then the man with the slow voice spoke. "The largest mackerel in the sea is the King Mackerel, I've seen him."

"It would be hard to see him, and he swimming."

"He was partially decayed when I saw him."

"He was dead?"

"He was. It was in the County Kerry I saw him. It was after he was sent to the analyst."

"Who sent him to the analyst?" I said.

"Well, there was two men there and they sent him. The two were standing on the beach of the sea and they saw this object rising outside on the water and they saw it dashing toward them, and they lay down and hid. They hid from it and it came along and it was nearing their side. It was a fish. They saw that at last. And with the force it was swimming it ran inland on the shore, something about eight or ten yards. And the two men ran at it and they threw themselves down on it, and when they looked about there was two seals coming right in the track of it—after this fish."

"Then it had the two seals beat?" said Patrick Sean.

"It had. And when you saw the size of it you'd understand. Well, anyway, the two Kerry men had never seen anything like it and they sent the fish to be analyzed, and by the time it was analyzed and back it was useless. It was a King Mackerel. And if they hadn't sent it to the analyst, if they'd cut it up and cured it fresh there weren't any two houses in the parish that it wouldn't supply for a twelve-month."

"What would be the weight of it?" said the young man.

"I forgot what was the weight of it, but it was a good many hundredweight. The Kerry men thought it was a King Salmon. But it was not. The analyst made out it was a mackerel—a King Mackerel."

There was a silence. Then Sean Patrick picked his ashplant up from the floor, stared at the head of it and said, "I saw the King of the Seals myself."

"The King Seal," said the man with the slow voice, and one knew he was impressed.

"I did. And there were two of a crew with me in the boat when I saw him. And he was the biggest seal I ever saw, as big as any cow. He rose up out o' the sea alongside of us, and there was limpets and periwinkles growing on his cheeks and his head with the height of age."

"Is that so?" said the man with the slow voice.

"And I was one day fishing and if there wasn't a thousand million seals there in the sea around the boat there wasn't one. There is one day in the year, you understand, when they send the seals in thousands from along the coast to choose their king. And they disperse to their own places after. I saw them. And this king. I remember well his face, for 'twas like the face of an old man."

That made the young man laugh. As he stared at Patrick Sean and laughed again, I thought he was comparing this old round face with one he had seen looking up from the sea, but he said he had seen one with whiskers like Pat Finney's. That was what made him laugh, he said, but Patrick Sean did not even smile.

"The eyes of a seal," said Michael the Ferry, "are the very same as a man's eyes."

"He's something like a man in his ways," said the man with the slow voice. Now Patrick Sean laughed and banged with his ashplant again. "He must be, when he can drink rum."

"You are still waiting for that story," said the man with the slow voice.

"I am of course."

"Well there might be no harm in it here in the house," said Michael the Ferry.

"I am disposed to tell it," said the man with the slow voice, "because this man never heard it and we are alone here now. But, you must remember," he said, turning to me, "that I'll only tell it as it was told to me. I don't know is it true or not. And if you will excuse me, I'll omit the nomenclature of the party concerned, because I have no wish to cause offence to anyone."

"That's only right," said Patrick Sean.

"Oh there's no harm in it here in the house," said Michael the Ferry.

"Well," said the man with the slow voice, "it was something the same as what happened to your ancestor Michael—him with the waistcoat. It was on the occasion of a Fair Day in Belmullet. It was a patron day and the whole country folk used to assemble on this particular day, but there lived on the coast of Kilgallaghan in Erris a man whose intention it was to go to this Fair. And in those days traveling to Belmullet was chiefly by curragh. When he came to the beach on this morning to go in the curragh, as previously arranged by him with his neighbors, he found that all the curraghs had left for Bellmullet town for the Fair. And there was nothing for him to do. He sat there very disconsolate and sat on a rock. But he wasn't long sitting there until a huge seal puts up his head out of the water, almost at his feet, and addressing him by his Christian name he said to the man—the seal said, 'I see, my poor man, you are late for your curragh this morning.' 'I am indeed,' said the man, 'and I'm sorry and I don't know what to do now and I won't be able to go to the Fair. There's no way of getting to Belmullet unless I go by road around by the coast and by the time I reach Belmullet it'll be night, so I suppose there's nothing for me to do now but to get back home and make the best of it.'

" 'Very well,' said the seal. 'Do you know what you'll do? I'm going to Belmullet too, going to the Fair.'

" 'You're going to the Fair at Belmullet?' said the man to the seal.

" 'Yes, indeed I am.'

" 'Well, indeed, you'll cut a nice figure at the Fair.'

" 'Never mind that,' he said, 'I'm going to the Fair and I'll be at the Fair, and what I would suggest to you now is just get up on my back and I'll carry you to Belmullet. Don't be afraid, you won't be drowned. Nothing will happen, I'll guarantee you that.'

"The seal persuaded the man anyway to get up on his back and he did so, and off the seal started on his voyage to Belmullet up Broad Haven Bay. They weren't long out on the sea until they were joined by a shoal of seals—a whole lot of seals. The man says to the seal, 'Where are all these seals going?'

" 'Oh, we're all going to the Fair.'

" 'My God,' says the man, 'such a lot of seals going to a Fair.'

" 'Don't mind, we'll be there.'

"They were going up along until they reached the harbor or the estuary of Inver, which was somewhat narrow, and the people on both sides of the shore were amazed to see this man going along with the upper part of his body up out of the water. And the seal says to him, 'Why are those people watching us?'

" 'Well I suppose they're watching me,' says the man on the seal's back, 'thinking it an extraordinary thing to see a man like me with only the half of him out of the water. They're surprised.'

" 'Oh well, we'll soon see about that,' said the seal. So the seal set up a magic fog, or what is called in modern parlance a smoke screen, and the natives could see no more seals, couldn't see the man again. And under cover of this fog they reached Belmullet Pier, and the man got off the seal's back at the pier and stepped ashore, but when he turned round to thank his benefactor the seal, the seal had disappeared, and instead of a seal he saw a fine gentleman standing beside him. He kept looking around for the seal. Took no notice of the man.

" 'You're looking for something?'

" 'Well I'm looking for a seal.'

" 'Well you needn't look any more. I'm the seal.'

" 'Oh you're the seal!'

" 'I am, yes.' They got into conversation. 'I am the man—I am the seal that brought you here.'

" 'Well now, as you did, the only way I can thank you is—would you mind coming up to the public house and I'll stand you a drink?'

" 'Very good,' said the man. 'I will.'

"They both walked up to the public house and went into the bar. 'Now,' says the man to the seal, or to the seal-man, 'what are you going to have?'

" 'Well I'll have the seaman's drink—a glass of rum.'

"So he took the glass. They both had glasses of rum, and when they had their drink finished they shook hands and parted, and he saw no more of the man or of the seal after that. That is the story that's told in Erris."

"Now would you be apt to believe that story?" said Michael the Ferry to me.

"I don't know."

And the man with the slow voice said, "There's a lot of people are disposed to disbelieve it and some of those skeptical people were disposed to think that he concocted this story himself, but others did believe it and do believe it yet."

Next day I crossed the ferry again, with Michael and two policemen, heavy men whose faces leapt alive when they heard I had been in the South, in County Cork, their home. With sudden animation they spoke about friends and villages there like men long exiled in a bleak and foreign land. While they were on their rounds, Michael walked with me along the shore to the Beach of the Seals, a pleasant stretch of yellow sand below the graveyard.

"My father saw sixty seals here on the day of a funeral," he said.

"Tell me."

"It was his father's funeral. It is here we land the coffin."

"What happened?"

"I'll tell you again."

"But I shall leave today."

"I'll tell you the day you come back. You will be welcome any time."

"Thank you."

We climbed a bank and a stone wall and went to look at his wife's grave. We did not speak in the graveyard, but as soon as we were on the road, walking back toward the public house, he began to talk.

SOME OF THE PRIESTS OF IRELAND, IN THE EARLY days, escaped from the world as they knew it by sailing in curraghs to the North, and many of the remote places where they found refuge are named after them. Papa Stour—"The Great Priest"—is an island, about two miles long and one across, to the west of the mainland of Shetland. Its coast is cut deeply by the sea, violent on the Atlantic side even in summer, and swift like a river in spate on the lee-side, where the tides race through the Sound of Papa. I crossed the Sound of Papa in a drifter with six dealers who were going to buy sheep and cattle on the island.

The annual sale is held by the wall of the churchyard, on a green hill above a sandy bay. Six or seven bullocks and old cows were teth-ered there and about two hundred tiny Shetland sheep were mewed, unhappily bedraggled, in pens against the wall, their wool tight and sticky, their delicate pink nostrils quivering, their horns warm to touch in the rain, their eyes afraid, staring at the people who stood in groups waiting for the auctioneer to start. He started with an Angus bullock.

I was leaning against a sheep pen absently watching this black creature as it strained against the woman who held it by a rope, its hoofs dug obstinately into the glistening grass, its tail lashing slowly, its eyes turned now to the sky, now to the half-circle of children, men and women who laughed and spoke, eager as at a festival, brightly dressed with scarves, broad checks or yellow oilskins, listening to the auctioneer only when the price grew high and pressing closer to him then, as he stood watching, chanting, watching for the almost imperceptible movement of a finger or an eyebrow used to indicate a bid. I heard him chant, "Twenty-seven I'm bid, twenty-seven I'm bid, twenty-seven and a half I'm bid, and a half and a half and a half I'm bid. Twenty-eight I'm bid . . . "—but as soon as I was more attentive a voice beside me said, "We used to have good cattle."

"That one looks good," I said.

"A fine lump of a bullock yon," he said, "but we had the best on the island one time, the wife and I."

"Not now?" I said.

"Not now."

"Why's that?"

"Two old people. We canna manage now." He looked at me and smiled. I saw he was amused and half ashamed by what he had caught himself saying. I liked him. He was very tall and narrow and though he stooped a little, his face, so alert and hard and ready to laugh, made him seem young until one saw him walking.

"Ye are no' buying cattle the day?" he said.

"No, no. I just came on a visit."

"Ye're from the South?"

"Yes." I told him about my parents and about my childhood at Nairn. I told him some things I remembered of Derbyshire and London.

"But ye were born in Scotland?" he said.

"No. I was born in India."

That amused him.

"And ye found your way to Papa Stour," he said. "Ye lost no time." He called a younger man to him with a sideways nod of his head. "I have a stranger with me, Gideon, and he was born in India."

"It is bad day for the sale," said Gideon. "The lambs look thin with the rain."

The auctioneer went on chanting.

"I sailed with the Royal Mail when I was young," the old man said. "There were no nicer men in the crew than the Indians. But no matter where ye were born, ye'll end where your lot is," he said, and he looked at me as if he wished me to say still more about myself.

I said, "I have come to Papa Stour because I believe the gray seal breeds here."

"The selchie? Aye, he does. There's plenty o' them in the caves alow the cliffs," said Gideon. "And on the Ve Skerries plenty more," the old man said.

"Could I get out to the Ve Skerries?"

"Ye'll see nothing there but cormorants and every kind of sea bird."

"And seals?"

"Seals at low tide," Gideon said, "but 'twould be hard to land there in weather the like o' this. Those Skerries are little more than crags standing out o' the sea. And they are three mile westward o' this. If ye walk beyond the dykes ye'll see where they lie."

"How much did yon black bullock fetch?" the old man said.

"Thirty-two pound."

"He's worth more."

The auctioneer had moved away taking most of the people with him. He chanted on.

"Did ye wish to go shooting the selchies?" the old man said.

"No. Just to look at them."

"There's no need to go as far as the Ve Skerries for that. They are all about this island."

"I have seen them come ashore as far as this," said Gideon.

"Aye, and as far as the center o' the island, aboon the Dutch Loch," the old man said. "But I think there is something wrong wi' them when they come far inland."

"You think it's when they're ill?" I said.

"There is something wrong, I'm thinking."

They spoke together in dialect and laughed. I found it impossible to understand them unless they were speaking directly to me in the careful English they reserved for strangers, and even then they pronounced the "th" like a soft "d" and used many words that I had never heard before.

The old man said, "We never used to kill them when we saw them far inland."

"Do you still hunt them?"

"Some does," said Gideon. "An odd time gif he wants a pair o' rivlins."

"I never see you in rivlins, Gideon."

"No. It's plimsolls I wear now."

"Did ye ever see a pair o' rivlins?" the old man said to me.

"I've seen shoes made of cowhide with the hair left on."

"Aye, that's rivlins, with the hair outside. But cowhide is too stiff unless ye cure it. The sealskin ones is full of oil. They're inclined to feel damper on the feet, but I like them the better, for they never will go hard."

"There's more wear in the cowhide," said Gideon.

"There's wear in the sealskin too—only that they'll soon give out if you walk in them below the mark o' the high tide."

"That's only a notion," said Gideon.

"Maybe."

When the sale was over, he asked me to his house for tea. As we walked toward it, the rain stopped and the sun made the hills and sea turn blue, in many shades. It was a sudden transformation like the change of a scene in a play.

The old man's name was Thomas Charleson. His son Gilbert was there, at home on leave from the Navy, a man of about forty, much like his father with an amused and easy air. Mrs. Charleson was gray and small. She sat beside me and smothered me with bannocks and oatcakes without saying very much. The room was bright, almost too clean for comfort, the table had been scrubbed daily for so many years that it was white, and two long strings of dried fish were hung across from wall to wall, gleaming like bits of silvery armor.

"I think Hamna Voe is your likeliest bay for the seals," said Thomas, after we have finished eating.

"Is it for photographs?" said Gilbert.

"No. It's . . ." I never know how to explain my obsession. "I am interested in them," I said. "I have heard strange things about them in Ireland and places." The two men laughed.

"There are strange things here," said Gilbert. He searched his pockets for a cigarette. There was only one. I had tobacco and cigarette papers, so I made one for myself and one for the old man. He examined it carefully.

"What is the name of the maker?" he said.

"Lucky Star."

"Na, na. I mean the maker o' the cigarette."

I told him my name.

"Ye are the first factory that ever was on Papa Stour."

"Did ye ever hear about the man that was lost on the Ve Skerries?" said Gilbert.

"No."

"Now there's a strange thing for ye. What was his name, Father?"

"I never kent his name. But the names o' the two selchies with him were Geira and Hancie."

Mrs. Charleson looked at me apologetically. "It is only a story," she said. "It's no' true."

"We canna tell is it true or no'," said Thomas. "It is long, long syne it happened."

"What happened?"

"It was when they used to hunt the seals on the Ve Skerries," said Gilbert.

"Well, I hunted them there myself," said his father. "But it was long before my time."

"This gentleman doesna want to fash himsel' wi' things the like o' yon," said Mrs. Charleson.

"There is one crag on the Ve Skerries," said Thomas, unperturbed. "There's a muckle wide hollow in the crag and it wasna hard to kill them in it. There'd be many o' them in it, and though some would escape and go into the sea, the men would likely get all they needed for skins. It wasna easy to land there, mind ye, and it wasna easy to win back to your boat when your work on the Skerry was done. Well, there was a crew from this island went out from Hamna Voe, beyond the dyke at the back o' the house here, and they managed to land on the Skerries in bad weather, and they attacked and stunned a number o' seals and skinned them. Ye'd no sooner stun your seal than ye'd set to and skin him, ye understand, because if ye left him there he might come to life and go back into the sea, while ye turned round about. 'Twas hard to be sure if they were dead or no', for it's very hard to kill them. And when ye'd skin them ye'd take off the fat wi' the skin, and put the fat and the skin into the boat, and ye'd leave the corpse there on the rock. Now, when this boat's crew had finished their work and loaded their boat with skins, there came suddenly a tremendous swell so big they thought it was like to drown the little island, so the men made a dash for the boat and all got safely in, except one. He was left on the rock. They tried to bring the boat near again, but the swell grew worse and the sky blackened, and try as they would they couldna win back to the rock, they couldna bring her near enough to let the other man jump in. So they left him. They left him there to die, maybe, o' the cold, or in the water maybe, for the waves could beat and wash him off the rocks yonder, and he hadna food nor covering except only his working clothes. They left him. Left him there to himself and went hame to Papa Stour. And the storm blew harder. There was a terrible sea that night and he was lonely and afeared.

"So mirtil came, but before it was quite dark he saw many seals coming back to the Skerry. 'Those'll be the ones that escaped us,' he said to himself. And at the same time the storm raged worse and he grew afeared he would be swamped, and the noise o' the wind was cruel, roaring and skreiching in his head, and along o't he could hear a wailing, a kind o' singing, like the voices o' the selchies. It was a lament he made out, when he made out the words, a lament for the loss o' their skins, for now they sang i' the lament that they could swim no more; they must live on land like men and women, they would ne'er again see the city o' coral and pearl that lies below the waves. And they described their city in this song—how the sea aboon them was like a sky, but pure blue and green, when they were hame—ten thousand times more beautiful than the sky above the earth. And they lamented their friends and brothers and sisters, every one by name—and the loudest o' the sobbing and lamenting came from a seal named Geira, and all the selchie folk lamented wi' her, for that her son would be parted from her for aye—he that had lost his skin and was condemned to live on land for aye. And his name, as they sang it, was Hancie.

"The man was now in despair. He stood up and looked at the sea, and it was wilder and more grumly fornent him, and he was cold and ootmoucht for want of a bite to eat. But when the selchies saw him they stopped their lamentations and at the start they were afeared. But Geira, the old mother, she went up to him and she spoke to him kindly. 'Ye are lost,' said she, 'and I have a sort of pity for ye in my heart, for ye can never go from here amongst your own. Never,' said she, 'will ye see again your own hearth stone, nor the folks that ye love, nor your mother, nor father, nor sister, nor brother. Nor your son,' she said, and looked at him gently. 'You will see nothing now except only the wild waves, and the black rock and the hard sky.'

" 'That's true,' said he. 'I am lost. I will surely perish here.'

" 'Well now,' said Geira, 'if I carry ye safe hame on my back, will ye give me your word to do what I ask you?'

" 'Aye,' said he, 'but I mightn't be able for what ye ask.'

" 'It's a peerie thing I ask,' said Geira.

" 'It micht be peerie and micht be great, but whatever it is I'll try to do it for ye, if it's within my power.'

" 'Then get on my back,' says she, 'and I'll swim wi' ye to Papa Stour.'

" 'I doubt is it better,' said he, 'to die here on the rock, or to die in the sea, for your coat is gey slippy wi' the water, and I micht fall off.'

" 'I'll keep ye safe,' said Geira.

" 'I dinna doubt ye,' says he, 'but in case I micht drown and the sea be too strong for ye, and the wind blow me doon frae yer back, will ye tell me what it is I must do.'

" 'I'll tell ye,' said she. 'Which of all the selchie men around ye now that are naked on the rock, which is the fairest o' them a', will ye say?'

" 'Him that is tallest, standing yonder and greeting, him with the black hair and white skin and red lips, him wi' the sorrow of an exile in his e'e, him that is starker and taller than them a'.'

" 'He is my son,' said Geira, 'and his name is Hancie. And if he is stark and tall, and if he is black and red and white, he is standing there now with the tears in his e'e, because never again will he be at his own hearth stone,' said she. 'Will ye fetch and find his skin,' she said, 'that he may travel through the water hame?'

" 'If it is in my power I'll fetch it.'

" 'Then put your legs astride my back.'

"But the wind and the waves were grumly yet and he was afeared.

" 'I hae here my gully,' said he to Geira, 'and if ye'll allow me, I'll cut holes in your skin, two for my hands and two for my feet. I'll be able tae grip ye that way, and I'll no slip into the sea.'

" 'If ye wish it,' said Geira, and he cut the four holes in her skin and slid on to her back and away. Away through the storm she swam then, and carried him with her safe to Papa Stour."

"That was it," said Gilbert Charleson, with a laugh.

"Wait yet," said his father. "I canna tell why she didna bring him a' the way to Hamna Voe. If he was anyway a big man, maybe she was tired, or maybe she didna like to come near to the house that was built on the shore o' the Voe. But anyway, she landed him on the other side o' the island at Akers Geo. A deep crack in the cliff," he said to me. "Ye can see the place for yoursel' if ye go beyond the dykes and over across.

"Now they used in those times to store the sealskins in what we call a skeo, a little stone house with no mortar, nor window, that was used for the curing o' fish. And this man went across the island in the night, when he landed. He walked down by the Dutch Loch and on to Hamna Voe. He made sure his comrades were sleeping and he went there to the skeo. And he chose out the longest and bonniest skin out o' a' that lay there and took it to the old mother selchie, Geira. It was the skin o' her son, Hancie, and away wi' that she swam."

He laughed and his wife looked at me.

"Such old stuff," she said, but Gilbert was laughing too.

"There was another man," said Gilbert, "and he was down getting bait at Hamna Voe, getting limpets off the rocks for bait, and he had a knife with half a blade to shift them. The blade was broken off, like. He looked round and he saw a seal on the stones o' the shore and he got between him and the water and stuck the blade in him. Well, the seal got away and the knife was in his side. Years after, this man was sailing on a ship and he was wrecked off the coast of Norway. He came into a house and they gave him his tea and he saw an old man in the chimney corner. "Did ye ever see that knife?" the old man said. There was a knife stuck in the wood o' the mantel shelf. He looked at it. Well, it was his own knife. It had only half a blade."

Mrs. Charleson clicked her tongue. "The old people were full o' superstitions," she said.

"Maybe," said Gilbert.

"And maybe superstition is right," said his father.

"Well," said Gilbert, "I think maybe the old people saw what we canna see. There no doubt, Mother, that your mother saw things. Now if ye think o' the trows, the little people—I believe there were some who could see them. And there's no doubt the little people were in Shetland one time. Ye can see the houses they lived in down at Jarlshof where the excavations are and the doors are only so high." He held his hand by his knee. "So maybe the people one time had the power to see what's hidden from us. In the hills there's something to be seen, I'm sure o' that. And on the sea."

"We believe what we believe," said his father, getting up and moving to the door. "And there's no way to ken is it right or wrong."

I went out with him.

On the rising ground behind the house I saw a high wall that stretched from north to south as far as I could see.

"Over that," I said. "Is that what you mean when you say 'beyond the dykes'?"

"Aye. A' the land across yon is rough grazing—and indeed it is rough. There's scarce a pick o' feed on it the now."

"Any houses over there?"

"Just one. And the roof is off it."

"I'll walk that way."

Beyond this dyke I was in another country, wild, silent and uneven. I had left slopes of green and yellow corn, rich grass and scattered houses, and saw before me a desert of stones and stunted heather falling steeply to the bay called Hamna Voe. Running inland through an opening in the cliffs, the sea forms here a wide harbor and is sheltered from the Atlantic, as though within a gate, so quietly and securely lapping that one might think it was a lake. The banks by its shore were cut all along into what the Shetlanders call "nousts," shallow beds in the ground the size and shape of boats. All except two were empty. There were "plantie cribs" too, small circular beds for cabbage plants enclosed by stone walls five foot high. A few of these had been planted. But there was no other sign of human activity. It was as though Hamna Voe had long been abandoned. When I walked there the evening was still and the sea almost motionless.

I came to two deserted watermills built over the bed of a stream, now dry, and walked out on a green promontory to the ruins of the house. It was built of red granite, roughly cut. I found the kitchen thigh deep in nettles and docks and stepped over a broken wall into the cowshed, from where I could see the whole of Hamna Voe, lying pale in the evening light below the far hill and black in the shadow of the cliffs nearby. I sat on the wall and made a cigarette. I heard a raven croak twice. I felt the autumn coldly on my face, but because this old cowshed had been lately used for dipping sheep there was a smell of dung as though the warm life of the farm lingered on.

The water was broken far out by the head of a seal, swimming slowly toward the shore. He sank and came up again close to me, gazed a long time in my direction and at last pulled himself on to the beach below the house. He heaved himself along the stones, using the muscles of his body like some clumsy snake, and came to rest not far from where I sat. He gazed at the cowshed for a while, and I could see his nostrils opening and closing as he breathed, but I kept very still and he did not see me. He lay down on his side, wiped his forehead with one sweep of his paw, like a man brushing sweat away wearily, scratched his chin, looked thoughtfully about him and closed his eyes. I guessed he was six feet long and, seeing the huge roundness and strength of his body, I thought it would be easy for him to bear the weight of a man. I rose cautiously after a while, intending to leave him undisturbed, but as I backed away he looked up sharply twisting his head to make sure, and giving out a long, heavy breath like a groaning sigh he rolled on to his belly and lumbered with all the speed he could make down over the rattling stones. He plunged into the sea and was at once transformed into a being of swift movement, graceful, strong and sure. Some distance out he stopped and turned, rose high in the water and stared at me. I looked at him. He did not move. When I reached the top of the hill he was still watching. I went down into the valley; I passed the Dutch Loch and climbed through the middle of the island till I came to Akers Geo, where Geira had put the man ashore.

The middle of the island is covered with small stones, almost bare, patched here and there with a scrubby kind of grass and with heather not more than an inch high.

There is no living creature there. But as you climb toward the cliff's edge on the Atlantic side, the land becomes vividly green with close-cropped grass, sliced in many places by ravines called "Geos," where the sea roars inland without warning, the plateau being almost level till it reaches a sheer drop of several hundred feet; and here there are kittiwakes and shags, and little sheep, some black ones and many white, which scatter wildly whenever you come near. I walked by such places every day on Papa Stour. It was lonely and often sad.

The cliffs to the south of Hamna Voe by the place called Shepherd's Taing are red, like rusted iron girders standing upright close together above a huge and frightening chasm. At Akers Geo they are black and as I lay looking down, the water, rumbling and sucking under archways of rock, was very black. I spent much time trying to decide where best to climb the cliff if one was landed there, but the thought was giddy. I thought too of death in that place and once at night I dreamt that I was falling into Akers Geo.

Until my last day on the island I saw no man beyond the dykes, but on the last day, at sunset, as I was walking homeward by the edge of the Dutch Loch, Gideon appeared from behind me with a dead lamb on his back. I asked him how it had died. He did not know. Looking at the loch, I asked whether seals ever swam in fresh water. He thought not. I asked why old Thomas Charleson had said he would not shoot them when he saw them far inland.

"They are no' like the otter," he said. "It is right for the otter to travel across the land and in the sea, but when the selchie is on land Tommy Charleson wouldna care to go near him."

"He'd think it unlucky?"

"He'd think the creature might be something more than a seal."

"I saw one come ashore by the ruined house. Down there."

"Aye. Very like. Did he see ye?"

"After a bit, yes."

"They are very intelligent," he said. We walked on. When we came to Hamna Voe he stopped.

"We were out shooting them from the boat there at the mouth of the Voe," he said, pointing. "And ye see yon Skerry yonder, where the waves is breaking? Well, there was a mother and she had a small baby, pure white, and we wanted to get him for his coat. But she got the young one to climb on to her back and she swam with him out to yon Skerry. Well, we watched her. She'd go under the water and come up and always he, the little white one, was holding on wi' his hands. Well, she went wi' him to a place on that Skerry where she kent we couldna come wi' the boat—just the one place where the sea was wildest. We were watching her a long while. But no one of us would raise a gun at her."

By a piece of a wall, near the watermill, he laid the lamb down and took out his pipe.

"So ye were at yon house wi' the roof off?" he said, pointing with his pipe to the ruin.

"Yes. How long is it since people lived there?"

"A good while. There was a family o' crofters had yon."

"A lonely place to be."

"Aye." He lit his pipe and looked toward the ruin. "It was the only house beyond the dykes," he said. The land about us was now a mass without colour in the dusk. Only the sky and the sea showed light.

"They had great misfortune," he said. "They left the island at the end."

I asked him to tell me about them, but he picked up the lamb and we climbed the hill and crossed the dyke without speaking. At the door of the Charlesons' house he said. "I often heard the selchie babies crying—in the autumn time. On the Skerries yonder. There's no way to tell the sound they make from the sound o' a human baby."

There he left me and I went home.

Thomas Charleson and his wife were sitting by the stove.

"Ye'll have wandered a good piece o' the island," the old man said. I told him how I had met Gideon. When I spoke of the ruin he laughed and told me the name of the crofter who used to live there.

"Why was he so unlucky?" I said.

"He was a hard man to drive a bargain."

"He acted wrong," said Mrs. Charleson.

"Well, I suppose," said Thomas, "we are a' made in our own fashion. It was over a wreck," he said.

I said, "I asked Gideon to tell me about it."

"He might be shy," said Thomas. "He is some kind o' great nephew to the man. And now if I tell ye about it, will ye give me your word no' to mention the name o' the crofter to any man?"

I reassured him.

"Well, a Norway ship came in a wreck to Hamna Voe," he said. "And this man bought her timbers off the captain, but they had atween 'em a sore dispute about the price. The Norway captain thought it wasna fair, but, being stranded, he took whatever the crofter gave him—and away with him to the mainland, and his crew along with him. But he was angry, and the last thing he said to the crofter was—he held up his hand and 'Ye will regret this,' he said. Well, every year after yon, in the wintertime, a seal came into Hamna Voe and up fornent the house, and he held up his flipper above the water, and that very night a cow would die.

"Every winter it was so, and always it was the cow in the last stall near the water that died. He got to ken it would be that one, and every year he put his poorest cow into that stall. When the time grew near he would hide himself wi' his gun, but the gun would misfire. He never shot the selchie and he lost a cow each year until he went from Papa Stour."

"It's no' so long since that happened," Mrs. Charleson said.

"It would be a hundred years syne."

"Or maybe less," said Mrs. Charleson. "It happened in the lifetime o' a woman we all know. She died in 1914 and she was eighty-four."

"Well, that could be a hundred years," said Thomas. "She used to tell me the seals were Finns—Norway Finns."

"There was no truth in that," said Mrs. Charleson.

"There was truth in the crofter's cows dying."

"Aye. But a lot o' those other stories is lies."

"We think it is lies," said Thomas. "But it was true some time. It happened some time. All those things happened."

ON THE QUAY AT KIRKWALL, IN THE ORKNEY ISLANDS, over one hundred miles south of Shetland, I watched an excited crowd of country people disembark from a steamer called *The Earl Thorfinn*. I was talking with a man who had worked in this harbor all his life. As we watched the crowd jostling on the gangway he told me they came from the North Isles of Orkney and of how when he was young the townspeople of Kirkwall would gather on the quay to meet them and make fun of them, greeting them with catcalls and mock fights. As the ship drew near, the passengers would shout "Starlings!"—their derisive name for Kirkwall men—and the Kirkwall men would answer with nicknames long established for the people of each island. The Shapinsay people were called "sheep"; the Stronsay people "limpets"; the Papa Westray people "dundies," which means "weak cod"; the Eday people "scarvs," an Orkney name for cormorants; the Sanday people "gruellie bellies," or eaters of gruel; and the islanders of North Ronaldsay, the most northerly island of all, were known as "seals" or "hoidies," hoidies meaning the hides from which they make their rivlins.

The island of North Ronaldsay is shaped rather like a hide with a foreleg where the lighthouse stands, one hind leg at Nouster and the other at the Point of Burrian. It is about five miles from corner to corner and at the widest place two miles across. It is entirely surrounded by a drystone wall and its beaches are populated with a breed of sheep now rare—the Orkney Native, a scraggy creature, long in the leg and neck, goatlike and wild, but with fine wool like the Shetland. As I walked on the beach at low tide I was surprised to see these creatures wandering on the rocks, some of them far out on promontories with the water swirling round them, some even wading in the sea to reach a new patch of seaweed, which, except at lambing time, is their only food. At the Point of Burrian I saw in the distance what I took to be a group of them lying down among the tangle, but these rose as I came nearer and plunged splashing into the sea. They were seals. In their varied, indefinite colors, the Orkney sheep resemble the Atlantic seals, which are only gray by name. Most of them are mottled, some are gray, some black, some foxy red, some almost white. On a grassy lane, where I walked inland, having climbed the wall, I found a big ram tethered by the foreleg. He had fawn and olive markings and his horns were like dark amber. He was very much afraid of me, straining wildly at his rope. Farther on I met a woman spreading washing on a wall. She was the tallest woman I have ever seen.

"Good evening," I said. "Is it going to keep dry?"

"I think so. I hope so. I've putten these stockings out three times and the rain came on them." Some long gray strands of hair blew across her face in the wind. Pushing them back, she held a hand to her head and looked seriously at me with dark eyes.

"Ye are a stranger," she said. "I've no' seen ye before."

"Yes, it's my first time here."

She turned suddenly, put her hands to her mouth and shouted. "Osie! Osie! There's a stranger, Osie!" I picked up a stocking she had dropped and gave it to her; she held it toward the sea. "Ye came yon way?" she said.

"Yes. I was walking on the beach. I was having a look at the sheep."

"Such a day to be walking in the wind and rain." She spoke very quickly.

"It's not so bad now."

"Well, well. Come into the house and rest yerself. Here's Osie.

Now!" She found stones to lay on the rest of the washing and led the way into the house. "He came up from the shore," she said to Osie. "I didna see him till he was close by."

"I saw the selchies shifting from the rock below," said Osie. "I was wondering what it was disturbed them."

"They're not a bit afraid of the sheep," I said.

"Na, na. But the sheep keep away from them, mind ye."

Osie Fea was almost as tall as his wife and although he was over eighty he walked well without the help of a stick and worked every day at the lobster pots or on his croft. Except for long sidewhiskers, still tinged with red, which gave him the look of a pirate out of some old book for children, his face was newly shaved, so glistening and red that when he took his cap off and undid his collar stud, showing white skin where his forehead and neck had escaped the weather, one might have imagined he was wearing a mask. A strong blue eye shone out of it above wide cheekbones. The other was blind and crumpled. But this one eye, a nose large and hooked, and chin shaped finely gave to his face the qualities of strength and penetration. Even with his jacket off his shoulders seemed abnormally broad, and his chest where it showed above a singlet was covered with red hair.

"I suppose," said Osie, pulling out a high straw-backed chair for me to sit on, "ye never in your life saw sheep the like o' those?"

"I never knew that sheep could live on seaweed."

"Well that's what the wall is there for—to keep them off the land. Nobody can mind the time it wasna there. Ye see, we need a' the grass on this island for the cattle, and the crops take up the rest, so the sheep must feed on the seaweed. And it's good. Ye'll no find the same diseases wi' these sheep as wi' the Cheviots or Leicesters, and there's no dipping to be done."

"I noticed a lot of dead ones—old corpses along by the wall."

"Aye. Some might die lambing, and the sea drowns one or two, especially at a time like this when the Lammas Stream brings the tide up to the wall." He meant the flood tides of August.

"I was watching them there," I said. "It seems they're not afraid to go into the sea."

"It's bred in them. I've seen them when they think they are in danger. In a narrow place below the house here, I've seen a big sea running at them against the wall, and they kent rightly what to do. They all stood close together and they let the sea break over them. Then ran when the wave went back. And if ye study them, ye'll see how they follow the way o' the sea. They'll shift round to the lea side o' the island afore a storm and they'll ken the run o' the tides afore ye'll ken it yersel'. They'll be down among the seaweed feeding as soon as the tide has left the least bitty o' it bare, and they'll be up by the wall afore the flood again to chew the cud. But nevertheless an odd one is drowned. And o' course we canna attend to them lambing. They are too wild altogether."

"I think the gentleman would be more interested in the southern sheep," said Mrs. Fea, politely. "I have a fine Cheviot ewe tethered out in the lane. Would ye no'?" she said. "Would ye no'?" she said again, but I was listening, puzzled, to a weird and mournful sound.

"I am sorry," I said. "I thought I heard something."

She stood still in the middle of the room with the teapot in her hand. "It is the selchies," she said. "I dinna care to listen to them crying."

Osie laughed. "Ye should be used to them by now," he said. "Ye've lived beside them a' your life."

"There's times I wouldna heed them any more than I'd heed the cock crow in the morning and there's times—"

"Did ye never hear yon sound afore?" said Osie to me, interrupting.

"Yes. I've heard it—often. But I'm never sure at first what it is."

"There's whiles it sounds human," said Osie. "There's something unco strange about the selchie. Did ye ever look close at their eyes?"

"Not very close," I said.

"They are able to weep," said Osie. "There's no other animal does yon."

"And they'll kiss one another," said his wife. "I wonder Osie, is that true?" She laughed.

We sat at the table and had tea.

"There is one thing I mind," said Osie, "and that's how we never could abide to look into the eyes o' a selchie if we was going to kill her. She'd look back at us wi' the eyes o' a person. She'd be afraid."

"But wouldn't it be the same with any animal?" I said. "With a bullock or a sheep, you can tell if he's afraid."

"Maybe. But that's no' what I mean. The selchie has eyes with every shade and light. Vex her and she'll show it to ye wi' her eyes alone, please her and she'll look softly. She'll change as quick as a woman. I often thought maybe it's because she's so awkward on the land wi' her body. God's given her no way else to show herself when she's on land. Ye'd ken what I'm talking about if ye saw one afraid."

"Yes."

"I was out on the shore last year and there was a young one in a pool and the boys had been stoning him. They stunned him, but he came alive and made for the sea close by me. He kent well he could come by me and take no harm."

"And you an old seal-killer!" the woman said. "How would he know to trust ye?"

"I never killed a young one," said Osie. "It was my brother's wife had the young one killed. There is six pints of oil in a young one, as much as ye'd get in an old one, and he's easier to take, but even when I made my living by them, I wouldna take a young one."

"It wasna for the oil she had him killed," said Mrs. Fea. "It was for rivlins."

"Aye. Well, cowhide was dear at the time."

"It was misfortunate," said Mrs. Fea to me. "She never lived to wear the rivlins from that skin."

I said, "How was that?"

"Och, 'twas a coincidence," said Osie. "But ye ken how folk will talk."

"Well now," his wife said, "it was yourself was talking."

"Aye. Well I kent it was wrong." He held his cup halfway to his mouth and put it down again. "She persuaded me to flay the young seal," he said, frowning at the tea. Then raising his hand toward me he spoke with hard insistence. "I told her—I said to her, 'Have noth-

ing to do wi' it. Ye were wrong to ask the lads to stone that little seal,'
I said, 'and I'd be wrong to flay him.' I said that. But the price o' the
cowhide was dear. I flayed him. She died afore the rivlins were
made. That was all there was about it."

"Take something more to eat," said the woman.

She cut pieces from a flat, circular bannock baked from the dark
flour of "bere"—a small grain much like barley—and we spread it
thickly with "crowdie," a sort of cream cheese.

"If yon's your first bere bannock," she said, "ye are no' like a
stranger the way ye go to eat it."

I found it very dry, but liked its unusual flavor and told her so.
She laughed.

"There was once a stranger begging at some door," she said. "And
the woman gave him a whole one heaped well wi' crowdie. Well,
what d'ye think? He ate the crowdie and gave the bannock back to
her. 'There's your plate, ma'am,' he says, 'and thank you.' "

"The way some o' the women bake, ye wouldna blame him," Osie
said, and the tension was gone from his face.

We were still at the table when the door opened and a man
walked in, shaking drops from his cap on to the floor, his oilskins
glistening from the wet.

"Good evening, Mrs. Fea," he said.

"The washing!" she said, with her hand to her mouth. "I beg your
pardon, Jimmy, but I'm all day running in and out wi't."

"Leave it out. Leave it out. It couldna be wetter."

Mrs. Fea got up from her chair and dwarfed him. "We have a
stranger here," she said.

"Aye. I've seen you the day," said Jimmy. "Ye was down on the
shore."

"Yes. I didn't see anyone else there."

He pulled the black oilskin over his head and hung it on a nail.
He moved and spoke violently.

"He's wondering where you're from," said Osie, smiling.

"I live in London now," I said.

"In London?" said Jimmy. "It's a long way from there to North

Ronaldsay. What brings him here?" he said as though I was not present. "What is he? Let him go home."

"Now, Jimmy, please!" said Mrs. Fea. "Conduct yerself." She pushed him down by the shoulders into a chair.

"Are ye looking at the way we do things in North Ronaldsay?" he said. "We want no changes here."

"I'm no' so sure o' that," said Osie, with good humor. "We could do wi' a new pier."

"What brings him from London?"

"Never mind him," said Mrs. Fea to me. "There's no harm in him."

"Let him go home." It was hard to tell whether he was really angry.

I said, "I had to leave London to get away from the Orkneymen there."

"Orkneymen in London?"

"It's full of them."

"Orkneymen in London!" He began to laugh. He waved his cap and shouted.

"Most of them are from North Ronaldsay," I said. "And nearly every one is a policeman."

He roared with laughter, tipping back his chair. "And what brings them to London?"

"I don't know."

"No man got anything there," said Jimmy, "nor on this island neither, except the six by two. I dinna care who ye are, that's a' ye'll get."

"Jimmy's a fright," said Mrs. Fea. "I'm sorry."

"It's easy to put you down," he said, still laughing and pointing at me. "But a hell o' a job to take you up again. Ye canna burst out till Judgment Day and very few will burst out then."

"No' you nor I," said Osie.

"I'm no' so sure," said Jimmy, serious again. "I have a fair chance, Osie."

Again I wondered whether he meant what he said, and now that he was silent in a daydream my mind began to search back through my travels wondering whether others had resented my arrival, but been too polite to say so. Jimmy's attack had brought me near to him. We were foreigners on equal terms.

Mrs. Fea had gone out to fetch the washing. As she opened the door with her arms full the wild voices of the seals, clearer this time, distracted me again. She saw me turn to listen.

"Never heed them," she said, and closed the door. "Jimmy, here, had a pet one. Did ye no', Jimmy?"

"Aye."

"He was quiet was he no'? I never heard him cry the like o' yon."

"He was quiet around the house. But I have seen him sitting out on the rock below and crying that way by himself. Gin I went to call him he'd come ashore."

"He was friendly like a dog," said Osie.

"He would follow the boat and he'd try to follow me on land. But he never was contented in himself."

I said, "Did he want to go back to the sea?"

"Och, he had me annoyed, the creature, how he couldna make up his mind. But we never closed him in."

"He was like yourself," said Osie.

Jimmy raised himself in his chair and leaned forward.

"How like me?"

"When ye was at the Greenland fishing, ye was yearning to be back on the croft, and the second day home, ye'd be restless."

"Aye. Aye," said Jimmy. "The very same. Well, ye ken, Osie, I tried every way to put that selchie back into the sea."

"He got some class o' a disease," said Mrs. Fea. "I mind that well. He would be bleeding."

"Aye. He got sores and that's what decided me to get rid o' him. But it wasna a disease, Margaret. It was that he wore the skin o' his belly away wi' clambering up the road to the house yonder. And back to the sea and up to the house again and back again. He was tormented, Margaret. But would ye believe this? I rowed him five mile out and I put him in the tide race, where the tides might carry him

further, but he was home by morning. And one time I took him to
the Skerry and laid him in the rocks where the other selchies lie. No
use. No use. He came home."

"It was your wife he was after," said Mrs. Fea.

This amused them very much. Jimmy was rocking in his chair
again, his mouth wide open toward the ceiling.

"He never was discontented while ye was away at the Greenland
fishing," she said. Jimmy appeared to be in pain, but she had no
mercy on him. "Did ye ever think to look at the hands o' your
bairns?" she said, and his chair fell backward, pitching him on to the
floor.

When peace was restored to the room, Osie saw that I had not
understood the laughter.

"It was aye a joke wi' the women," he said, "that if their men neg-
lected them, they'd away to the selchie folk for comfort, or if a husband was unfaithful they'd do the same."

"And the children?" I said.

"Their hands were webbed," shouted Jimmy, pitching about
again.

"Na, na," said Osie. "But a kind o' horn grew on them."

"They were webbed like the selchie's paw!"

"That's no' true. I ken that family well and the fingers are like
yours and mine." To prove his point, he mentioned the name of a
family and of the island where they lived, but later he asked me not
to repeat the names. As soon as he spoke their name all laughter
stopped. They have, he told me, a hard growth on the palms of their
hands and on the soles of their feet, which handicaps them in their
work.

"It is some kind o' skin trouble," said Osie. "It has nothing to do
wi' the selchies. I am only telling ye about yon because it is supposed to be how this saying o' the women started."

"It was supposed to be that the fingers and toes were webbed,"
said Mrs. Fea. "The horn grew when they cut the web away."

I said, "But why do you talk of that family? What happened to
start this idea?"

"It started wi' an Orkney laird. Or wi' his daughter, I should say."

Osie glanced at his wife and moved uneasily in his chair. He said, "There's no sense in talking more about it."

"About Brita, is it?" said Jimmy, leaning forward. "I like to hear it. It is uncanny," he said to me.

"There'd be no harm in it, would there, Osie?" she said. He did not answer. "Would ye like to hear about Brita?" she said to me.

"Yes, I would."

"Well, she was the laird's daughter long ago and gin she married, she was a long while afore she had a baby. Folks say she married hasty."

"That's no' the beginning," said Jimmy.

"Wait yet. When her mind was set on the marriage she wouldna bide till the waxing o' the moon. She married hasty, and the moon was on the wane."

She seemed unable to go on.

"Was that thought unlucky?" I said.

"Folk say it will make the marriage-bed barren. Maybe there's something to it. But anyway she paid no heed to yon. And then again, gin she fixed the hour o' the wedding, she wouldna wait on the tide. She was wed on the ebb o' the tide."

"That means the same thing, does it?"

"Aye."

"If ye study the ways o' the sheep here on the shore," said Osie, showing an interest now, "ye'd might begin to think there's something to it."

Jimmy thumped his chair. "Ye're no' giving us the start o't, Margaret," he said.

"Be quiet, Jimmy," I said.

"Well now, this laird," said Margaret Fea. " 'Tis about his daughter I'm telling ye. She was a bra' tall lassie, and she was bonny. She had yellow hair, like the straw o' the barley, and her nose was straight and her lips were red and her eyes were set far one from the other and blue. Folk said she was a Norway lass, from the old blood o' the laird, her father, and her name was Brita. The folk that kent her well said she had a loving heart, but she was stark and tall, and she had a proud way wi' her, and gif any man sought to look for her she'd break him and treat him wi' scorn. But she was the laird's daughter; she was bonny, and she had a right good tocher coming to her, and when the gentry kent about that they came from every island and from the South itself to ask her hand. But Brita would have none o' them. She was cold. She'd look at them wi' scorn and some had made long journeys for to see her, but she broke their hearts. She didna like to be chosen, d'ye understand. She wanted to choose for hersel'.

"Now her father, the laird, had a man tae work about the barn, and o' a' the servants o' thon great house it was this man she treated hardest. She was hard on a' wi' scolding and chiding, but this man was never left a minute's peace. Her eye was on him morn till night and her tongue was at him sharply. But it seems she'd set her heart on him. She loved him. She was afeared to tell her father. She telt nobody, for fear they'd be angered that she'd gi'en a thought to one so far beneath her, and for fear maybe that her father might stop the money that was to be hers when he died. So she locked up her love in her own breast and she treated the farm servant roughly."

"That's right," said Jimmy. "Ye have the start right now."

"A few years after," Margaret Fea went on, "her father the laird fell ill and died, and now when the funeral was over, and when she kent her tocher was safely her own, she went tae this man o' the barn and she told him to marry her. He did marry her—no delay about yon—and the gentry was vexed, the length of Orkney, and there wasna one county that didna hold a laird that thought to win her. Brita treated them a' wi' contempt, and she went her own gait. She made the best housewife ye ever saw. She looked well to the farm and the house, and managed a' the business well, and I believe her husband had little to say in thae matters, for she managed him well too." She said this with a glance at Osie and he smiled.

"I wonder was she taller than her man," he said.

"She was o' course," said Margaret. "But anyway for a few years a' seemed well except for there being no bairn. And folk were gey surprised to hear that she was happy when she'd made a match so far from her own class.

"But Brita wasna happy. It wasna long afore she was vexed and disappointed wi' her man. But, being proud like, she'd said nothing to anyone, for she kent well the answer they'd give her—especially the gentry, they'd laugh gif they heard it. 'She shaped her ain cloth,' they'd say among theirsel's, 'and gif the dress winna fit her, let her wear it.'

"Well, I winna tell ye what was wanting, but whate'er it was wanting, Brita felt the want bitterly. Now it wasna a hard thing those times when a man and wife couldna agree, for them to get divorced, for there was no such thing as law courts or the like o' that to trouble wi'. A' that was needed was the man and wife to go to the mainland of Orkney to the Kirk o' Stennes, and go into the kirk, and if one went out by the south door and the other by the north they'd be counted no more man and wife. They'd be free to choose for theirsel's again. But that would be public. It would be known to a' the Orkney folk. And Brita was proud.

"She wasna one tae sit down and greet over sorrow, so she rose up one day at early morning and went down tae the shore and sat on a rock, where she saw the black mark o' the high tide. She waited there or the tide did flow, and when the tide came high she shed seven tears into the sea. Folk said they were the only tears she ever shed. But she kent that was what she must do when she wanted speech wi' the selchie folk.

"Well, as the first blink o' dawn made the waters gray, she saw a muckle selchie swimming for the rock. He raised his head out o' the water alow her, and he says to her, 'What's your will wi' me fair lady?' So she likely telt him what was in her mind and says he, 'Come down again to this rock at the seventh stream,' says he, 'and wait for me. For it's only at the seventh stream that I can come in the shape o' a man,' says he to her, and away wi' him swimming."

"That's the now," said Jimmy, slapping his knee with enjoyment. "It's the seventh day o' the stream, the day."

"Ye'll find it's the fifth," said Osie. "If ye count back to Monday's full moon."

"No matter," said Margaret, and although I saw she wanted to go on I asked what she meant by "the seventh stream." They all answered together.

"The Lammas stream."

"The March stream."

"There's nine days o' the stream."

"Nine days o' very high tides twice in the year."

"It's the fifth day, the day, o' the Lammas stream," said Osie, and Margaret Fea went on.

"So when the seventh stream was come, she went down and he was there. And she met him by the shore for many years after. And it wasna for good they met so often, for when Brita bore her first bairn the fingers and toes o' the bairn were webbed like the paws o' a selchie. And the second bairn the same, and every bairn she had after. And the midwife clipped the webs between every finger, and between every toe o' each bairn, and many a clipping Brita clipped when they were growing up—for to keep the fins from closing together again.

"Aye, well," said Margaret, "that was the reason they used to give for these men wi' the horn on their hands and feet. Folk said they were the descendants o' Brita, and wi' a' the clipping that was done, the fins couldna grow their natural way, so they turned into this horn and grew out o' the palms o' the hands and soles o' the feet. That was the way o't. Now what d'ye say to yon?" She turned to me.

"It's a very strange story," I said. "So this is the time of year when they were thought to come ashore in human form."

"This and the March stream," said Osie.

"And Midsummer," Jimmy said. "My mother used to tell us how they changed to men and women on St. John's Eve."

Osie stood up with his back to the fire, and the shadow of his face, cast on the white wall by the lamp, was like a giant Punch, grotesque and strong.

"It's no wonder they were thought to be like us," he said. "For the seals and ourselves were aye thrown together in our way o' getting a living, and everything we feel, they feel, ye may be sure o' that."

"I wouldna care to be near them," said Margaret Fea.

"I have watched them," said Osie, "as near as I am to you. I have seen a mother out by the Seal Skerry when the sea was full o' wreckage. There was a ship wrecked out by and it was rough and this wreckage was tumbling her young one about so he couldna win ashore. I could see the anxiety gazing out o' her eyes like a woman's. The very same. The very same as a woman's."

"It must take a terrible lot o' fish to keep them alive," said Jimmy.

Osie sat down again. He said, "Are they no' entitled to it, living under God?"

"I'm no' so sure," said Jimmy, with a laugh. "I've heard a Shetland man say they are some o' the fallen angels. God threw them out."

I said, "In Shetland they told me the seals were Norway Finns." But they all denied this strongly. Margaret Fea shook her head.

"Na, na," she said. "The Finn men were real men. They came over from Norway and places the like o' that long ago. They came after fish in their canoes."

"There was nothing wrong about the Finn men," said Osie, "only that they had the power to cure the toothache and the eczema, and the redwater and the strangles and the like o' yon. That was how the people came to think they had magic."

"They could row nine miles with one stroke of an oar," I said, for I had heard that somewhere. The idea appealed to Jimmy and he began to speak, but Osie interrupted him.

"The Finn men were aye on the top of the water," he said, "but the seals were below. And what's below the water no man could tell."

"Was there no' a cow that came up from the water?" said Margaret.

"On this island. Aye. It canna be true, but there was supposed to be a creature in the water for every one on land."

"Was it supposed to be a real cow?" I said.

"Aye. Aye. A stranger cow appeared inside the byre wi' the other cows. This canna be true. It's a story. And she had grand calves. But I forget, now, was it a seal or another cow came years after to the door o' the byre and said:

> 'Break thee bands, Bora,
> Take wi' thee a' thee stora,'

and the cow went away to the sea again."

I did not understand the rhyme at first, but he explained it. "Break thy bands," that is, your halter. "And take with thee all thy store"—your young ones. Bora was the name of the cow.

"An old woman told me yon," said Osie. "Well, there was supposed to be cows and sheep and every animal there. But the seals were the people o' the sea."

I got up and began to say good-bye because it was late.

"I suppose ye'll be thinking," said Jimmy, "that the sheep I saw ye looking at the day were descended from a ram that came out o' the sea."

"It would explain their habits."

"How long will ye bide on North Ronaldsay?"

"I'm not sure."

"Well my advice is—shut your eyes while you're here and open them when you're on the sea again making for home."

Mrs. Fea shook hands with me.

"Come back again," she said. "And the next time I'll know ye. Man, man, ye frightened me walking that way, so quietly from the shore."

The sky had cleared when I left them and the great moon that comes together with the Lammas stream was flowing on the sea.

IN THE WINTER, YEARS AFTER MY FIRST VISIT TO THE Hebrides, I made for South Uist again, and on the evening of my arrival everybody asked me, "Are you going to the dance?"

I had landed on another island, on Benbecula, the island to the north, and, there being only one bus across the bridge to South Uist, I had made up my mind to miss it and call at the pub on the few people I knew. It was they who all said, "Are you going to the dance?" The wind that had torn at me while I walked to the house near the bridge grew into a gale in the evening as we sat drinking and eating. It carried with it rain and sand. It attacked the windows of that bar like one who was angrily shaking a locked door. It made men glance over their shoulders in the middle of what they had to say; it screamed; it made them shiver as they sat too hot by a fire; it shriveled them and planted on their faces a look of deafness and stupidity.

"If you are going to the dance," they said, "you can go by Alan Macrae's bus—the blue one."

"But you will have to go over the ford on foot," said one.

"The ford?" I was astonished.

"He means the bridge. It was a ford until the R.A.F. came here in the war."

"Aye. There's no need now to wait for low tide."

"And will you go?"

"Yes, I'll go."

"Macrae's bus will wait on you beyond in South Uist. It is a small, little blue bus. You'll see it standing there. Will some of you get on to the telephone to the house across the bridge and tell Alan not to move before this man is with him?"

"Is no one else coming?" I said.

"We'll come over by and by. We'll come."

They were at the house before me. I never discovered how.

I went by myself across the long bridge. The tide was rising and the sea seemed very close to me as I fought my way over against the wind. It was impossible to face the wind and breathe. For some moments it was impossible to walk. My ears were buffeted, my eyes streamed and the hard sand from the beaches cut the skin of my face and hands like miniature shot. Out of the confusion of sound, in the darkness, as I leaned with my back on the wind to rest, I thought I could sometimes distinguish the rise and fall of music, slow, like a pibroch, and sometimes I heard rocks tumbling heavily down. But nothing was clear. It was hard to distinguish the wind from the sea, and at the far side it was impossible to know where the sea ended and the land of South Uist began below the bridge.

Alan Macrae was dressed in an old khaki overcoat with a rope round his waist instead of buttons. I was his only passenger as we set out, but on the side-roads and rocky tracks of our long and winding journey to the dance we waited many times in deserted places where people came out of the darkness in two's and three's silently until the bus was full of talk and laughter.

The dance was held in a schoolhouse, where the largest class-room had been cleared of desks. Pipers and fiddlers, in their turn, sat on the master's dais at one end and the walls were lined with benches. On one side sat the men, most of them dressed in blue Sunday suits with cloth caps on their heads, on the other the women, many girls in bright dresses and several old women in black. The floor had been sprinkled with soap flakes to make it slippery. Two paraffin lamps hung from the ceiling. Their light was dim. They cast large circular shadows on the floor.

Early in the evening the room was quiet between dances, conversation went on in undertones, attitudes were easy like those of people resting at dinnertime in fields, but the first note of each dance was a signal for action, sudden and almost alarming until one understood what it meant. The men rose all at once and ran across the room with hands outstretched to seize the girl they wanted. As the boards shook with the clatter of their boots, four or five would collide by each of the more favored girls and the first hand to grab hers would win. The slowest or the weakest men would turn aside when they saw they were beaten and attempt to capture a partner from among the women who were left. I found it took practice and courage to achieve one's end. Modern dances and reels came alternately.

As soon as I came into the room, I was aware of one girl, tall, black-haired and full of health. There were many such, but she each time I saw her for a moment moving in the crowd affected me nostalgically and deeply. She was absorbed in herself and during the first dance we had together she only once looked at me and she did not speak at all. It was the custom to separate immediately after each dance, men and women walking quickly to opposite sides of the room, so there was little opportunity to talk, but later in the evening when the gale outside and the violence of the dancing and the music made the company more fluid, I went with her to the end of the room where people were standing in groups.

"Tell me your name," I said, and she answered in so low a whisper that I could not hear. When I told her mine she nodded and said, "I know," but because she was grown up now and was wearing lipstick, I still did not know who she was. She wore round her neck a white ribbon that disappeared beneath her jersey as though it held a locket.

I said, "How do you know?"

"I do remember."

"I didn't see you on the bus."

"There is no right road from our house."

"So you walked here?"

"I did."

Someone slipped and fell at the far end of the room. I looked round for a moment and when I turned to her again she was gone. But by now I had mastered the method of choosing a partner and I danced with her again.

The gale blew as hard as ever when we left the schoolhouse, and though I took her arm in mine it was she who led me with her good eyes and her knowledge of the stony darkness. We walked a long way and were at ease together. We reached the smooth, sandy grass and the sea when we got near it showed us light, but the thundering of it and the tearing of the gale made it impossible to speak. We were among the sand dunes when the hail began. She put her lips against my ear and said, "Come on," and ran.

With the hail beating on us we ran to the ruins of the Black House where first I had met her. We found shelter at the far end where the roof was good, and drying my hands on my shirt I got out cigarettes. There was some straw in the corner of the floor.

As I lit her cigarette I noticed the ribbon again.

"Is that a locket?"

"Will you light another match? I will show you."

I struck another and she pulled from under her jersey the Virgin Mary's bean.

I held it for a moment in my hand below her chin. "It hasn't gone black," I said.

"Why do you say that?"

"Because, when I last saw you, you told your grandfather you wanted it to go black."

"But there'd be no luck in it then."

"I know."

"Well, it is brown yet, isn't it? But do you know, there's one on the island, and a boy called Niall Mackellaig found it, and it is pure white like a shell out of the sea. I hope the ringboats come home safe."

"Is Niall Mackellaig on a ringboat?"

"He is. There wasn't much wind early."

"They are strong, big boats."

"I have sometimes heard it worse and they to come home safe. But those ringboats land in at Lochboisdale and we do have to wait till morning before we get word."

"Does your brother work the ringboats too?"

"Did they not tell you then about Angus?"

"I only arrived this evening," I said, fearing bad news.

"He's away to Glasgow, apprenticed to a joiner."

"Is that such a terrible thing?"

"It is a grand thing for Angus. But now it is very hard for me to leave home when I am the only young one there. And I do hope to go into service on the mainland. Tell me, were you ever in Glasgow?"

"I have been there often. I don't think you'd like it. Not for long."

"Why wouldn't I?"

"Too much hurry and clatter."

"But if I get married, I should like to have the electric. Tell me, did you ever see a gas stove at work?"

"I have used one, yes."

"They're grand things aren't they?"

"Yes."

"My aunt wrote to me from Glasgow about hers and she says they are grand for boiling the potatoes. You have only to put a match to them she says, and there's flames on them, that minute, as hot as a big fire."

"That's true."

"And quench the flames as quick? Is that true?"

"Yes. They are easy to work."

"Well, I think that's grand, don't you?"

I was going to tell her more about gas stoves, but as she spoke another piece of the roof fell in. The wind and the sea seemed suddenly louder and the hail smashed into the stones of our ruin. Some heavy thatch flew away and the rest sagged torn and dripping down into the room.

I said, "We had better go."

"Let us wait a while," she said, "until that hail does blow itself away."

"But the roof isn't safe."

"It is safe enough here in the corner, and if it does fall it is only light."

"Then let's sit down."

She moved away from me and began to sing a Gaelic song, slow and expressive of sorrow as so many of them are. I sat down on the straw.

"Have you any songs from Glasgow?" she said, breaking off.

" 'I Belong to Glasgow.' That's the only one there is so far as I know."

She came and sat beside me. "Sing it."

I sang the first line, out of tune.

"I don't like that song."

"Nor do I—even when it is properly sung."

"I heard it on the wireless," she said. "It's very old, isn't it? It is too old. You are not a great singer are you?" she then said.

"I can't sing at all. That song you were singing just now must be old."

"Oh, it is. My mother sings it. But I can sing 'The Dog in the Window' too. I heard it on the wireless."

"What is the name of your mother's song?"

"It has no name. It is very old. It is the song I like best of all the songs I ever heard."

"Sing it again."

"But you have no Gaelic," she said.

"You can tell me what it's about before you start."

"It is about a girl who was betrothed and her lover was unfaithful to her. It is very sad at the beginning, but at the end it is well for her. Are you wanting another cigarette?"

"Yes. Are you?"

"I am. Thank you."

Her eyes looked sleepy in the light of the match. I noticed that the hail had stopped, but said, "Go on."

"This girl was alone at the mountain shieling with her cows in the summertime. The girls used to stay there all summer when my mother was young. But before she left the glen this girl was betrothed, and she thought of her betrothed every night and morning, until one day a friend came and told her how she was like to lose him. He had found another girl in the glen, one that had a better dowry, and he had his mind made up to break the betrothal. So one day he climbed the mountain to her shieling. He came there to tell her what was in his mind. But when he saw her his heart would not allow him to tell her. He said his horses were astray on the mountain and that he had come to search for them. He said he was not able to pass by without looking in to speak with her. But she knew the truth, and as he turned from the door she sang."

"Yes?"

"She sang this song my mother has."

She sang it quietly and the wind still howled about us. When she came to the end she again said, "But you have no Gaelic. You do not understand the last verse."

"No."

"She sings all the verses until that one and she shows him by then that she knows about the other girl. But the last verse is his answer. He turns to her again and sings it. And he sings how he will come back to her, no matter how small her dowry may be."

We felt cold when we left the Black House, but outside it was dry, the gale had dropped a bit, and the clouds were split to show in ragged patches a moonlit sky. White horses shone and danced far out to sea and beside us, as we walked upon the sand, the breakers rose immensely, thundered, sucked and thundered down again. When we came near the gap in the dunes where we were to turn inland toward her house, we stood and watched, and standing close together each of us was solitary.

As we walked inland she said, "Do you believe is that song true?"

"In what way true?"

"Do you believe that when a boy has gone off with some other, his first girl would ever win him back?"

"She might."

"But do you think she would?"

I said, "They were alone on the mountain in your song."

"I think she would hardly win him back."

When we came to her house, I thought it too late to go in and see the old man, so I left her at the door and promised to come back next day.

"Where will you go now?"

"To Lochboisdale, to the hotel."

"To Lochboisdale is six miles."

"They are expecting me."

"Well, the night looks better now. You'll have news of the ring-boats in Lochboisdale. Come early tomorrow with news."

"I will. Good night."

"Safe home."

She went in and I walked back toward the sea. I had not enough energy to walk to Lochboisdale, so I slept with my overcoat round me in the ruins of the old Black House. When I woke the sea was quieter and the air still with frost.

I reached Lochboisdale soon after ten in the morning and was glad to see the ringboats at the quay. Their crews were complete in the bar of the hotel. I spoke to Niall Mackellaig and told him Mairi Finlay had been asking after him. He nodded and told me about the gale.

In the afternoon I went back to the Finlays' White House. It had not altered. Mairi's mother still seemed to spend most of her time breaking peats up and stoking the stove, and the old man Ronald Iain with his knotted brown face, sharp eyes and stiff body had not grown perceptibly older.

"I was vexed," he said, "when I learned how you were by the door last night and not made welcome."

"Mairi made me very welcome—but it was late. I had to go."

"She has no sense. With that wind and rain ye could have rested here the night."

"I hope she asked to bring you in?" said her mother.

"Of course she did."

"She has very little sense," said Ronald Iain, scratching his head.

"And what did you think of her, tell me?" said the mother. "She has grown a good piece since last you saw her."

"I didn't recognize her to begin with."

"She is tall," said her mother.

I said, "She's a beautiful girl."

"She is," said Ronald Iain, "and she's strong to work too. Will you believe me that? But by misfortune her head is filled with notions."

"She is only young. She is eighteen years," said her mother. "Did you find her quiet in herself?" she said to me.

"She talked quite a bit."

"I am glad of that."

"It is only at home she is quiet," said Ronald Iain, "and she has just the one thought in her head—to be away from home. And when she has the best offer she will ever have to be away from home, doesn't she turn round and refuse it?"

"Now, Father, I think we spoke enough about that."

"This man never heard it," said Ronald Iain.

"It has no interest for him. It is one little thing," she said to me, "where Mairi and my father have disagreed."

"It is no little thing when the whole of her life in years to come hangs on it," said Ronald Iain.

"That's what the poor girl will say herself."

The old man turned to me. "I have an offer for her from a strong farmer in the island of North Uist. He has twenty milk cows and the best farm of land in these islands, and he is well known to me. And she will not have him. Now, what do you think of that?"

"I think she's too young to get married."

"She has no father, mind you."

"Can we not leave this be for a minute?" said her mother.

"No father. And her brother Angus is away to the mainland . . . "

Mairi's mother put the corner of her apron to her eye and left the room.

"The woman doesn't like to hear me talk about it," he said. "The child Mairi was born a love child. Her father was off a Norway ship and there was never a penny got from him from that day to this. Without Angus there will be no one to work the croft when I am gone, and what shall she do then? It is not every man will marry a love child."

"I don't think you should worry about her. Things aren't the same now as they were when you were young."

"Indeed and they are not. I never heard such a carry-on as the young people make about marriage."

"I don't expect she's thought about it seriously."

"She has then. Hasn't she her heart set for the past year or more on this young boy that's with the ringboats, and he walking out with Calum Angus Campbell's daughter before our eyes? The women in my day had no such notions. Look at myself. Didn't I make the best marriage that any man made and I never saw my woman till the day of the betrothal."

"Did your father arrange it?"

"He did not. He was dead before that, God rest him. And I was living at home in North Uist at the time. I had word of a woman living in the south of this island, near to Lochboisdale, and I set out to ask for her on foot. I traveled the length of Benbecula and came to the ford, and when I crossed the ford I saw a woman working in the field beside the water. And she shouted to me. Now I was not inclined to stop, for I had another twenty miles to travel and I wished to be there before dark. But "I know where you're going," shouts this woman to me from the field. "And I know why you're going," says she. "And you have no need to travel a step further," she says. So I stopped with her there and I married her."

When he saw me laughing, he laughed too.

"It was like MacCodrum's marriage," I said. "Wasn't he from North Uist too?"

"Then you know how the Clan MacCodrum came to be?"

"I have heard a bit about it."

"Well, it did happen in North Uist," he said. "But it was many years ago. He was hunting cormorants when he found his wife. Is that what you heard about it?"

"I heard he was hunting the seals."

"Man, man. You're a terrible man for seals. You were on about those creatures the last time you came to see us, and that's—how many years is it now?"

The door opened and Mairi came in with her hair blown and tangled and a bucket of potatoes on her arm.

I said, "Good morning. It's a better day," or something like that, and I thought she was not going to answer, but she turned when she reached the other door and said, "There was a white frost this morning. It struck the potatoes at the head of the clamp."

I said, "I was in the bar at Lochboisdale this morning."

Ronald Iain said with exaggerated kindness, "Will you sit down with us, Mairi? This man has asked me about the Clan MacCodrum." But she went out of the room.

"So MacCodrum wasn't hunting seals," I said at once.

"I heard he was hunting cormorants on one of the small little islands," said Ronald Iain, "a kind of a reef. It was the fashion at that time for three or four men to go there from North Uist. One man would wait by the boat and the others would go up among the rocks to hunt the birds. So this night it was MacCodrum that stood to watch the boat. He found shelter for himself in a cleft o' the rocks and 'twas well after midnight when he looked down on the strand and he saw a number of people that were there, strangers to him, and they taking up, each one of them, a skin from a heap of skins that was there. They put on the skins and in a moment they were changed into seals and they dived into the sea. And when they were in the sea he went to the place where the skins were and he saw one fine sealskin lying there, and took and hid it under his coat. He returned to the place where he was. Well, he wasn't long there when a woman appeared before him.

" 'Give me,' said she, 'my clothes.'

" 'What clothes?' said he.

" 'My skin.'

"And he said, 'What has left you later than the others?'

" 'Oh,' said she, 'I am the daughter of the King of Lochlann and had a longer way to come, but you give me my clothing and I shall join them.'

" 'Indeed,' said the man, 'I won't give it you at all, but I shall bring you to my own home and you will be along with me,' he said.

" 'Oh,' said she, 'give me my clothes.'

" 'You'll not get them.' And he took off part of his own clothes and put them on her.

"The other men came back and they wondered where he had got the beautiful woman.

" 'By the Book,' said he, 'this is a woman I have found, and I am glad she is going with me.'

"The hunters put the cormorants into the boat and he hid the skin as well as he could, and when they reached home, 'Do you go home now,' said he, 'and I will attend to the boat.'

"But they said, 'We must divide the birds first.'

"So they divided the birds and the others went home to their homes. He saw to the boat, and when he saw to it, 'We shall now go home,' said he.

" 'Oh,' said she—'I'd rather if you gave me my skin and I'd do anything you ask me.'

" 'Oh you won't get it at all,' said he.

" 'If I see my skin I shall get it,' she said 'and I'll be as I was before.'

"He went home and hid the skin and he dressed her up and she was a beautiful woman."

Mairi came back into the room. Her grandfather went on without looking at her.

"They lived together a long time and they had many children, mostly boys, and were very happy together, and always he kept the skin hidden. But she told him again and again to keep it in a dry place and to let no dampness spoil it.

" 'For,' said she, 'although I am happy here I'd rather be where I was before.'

" 'Oh the skin is safe enough,' said he, 'as safe as if it were on your back in the waves of the sea.'

"He changed the hiding place of the skin from year to year and he preserved it as well as he was able. It was not an easy thing for him to hide it, you will understand, for the children were growing up in years, do you see, and he couldn't turn without having them around him. And always it was she made the children go with him.'"

Mairi was by now absorbed in the story. She rested her chin in her hand and watched her grandfather. He looked at me and went on.

"But this day they were stacking corn," he said, "and didn't one of the boys see his father coming with a sealskin and putting it into the heart of the first stack that they made. The boy wondered greatly why his father put the skin into the stack. But the stack was made and others after it, and when the work was finished the father had to go away and leave the mother and children alone at the house.

"She would question the children every day to know did they see anything like a skin about the place. Well, she was one day baking bread, and, 'Indeed, I did,' said the eldest boy. 'I saw my father put a beautiful, beautiful skin into the heart of the first stack of corn.'

" 'You saw him?' said she. And she was delighted. She went on with the baking as quick as she could bake and when the baking was over she made everything ready for the father to come home.

" 'Well,' said she, 'I am now going away from you. You will not see me again if I get the skin.'

" 'What are you saying?' said the children.

"She went to the stack of corn. She took the stack to pieces till she came on the skin.

" 'Oh,' said she. 'This is my own skin and you will go down with me to the shore and as long as I live I will keep you in fish every day.'

"So they went along with their mother to the shore. She took off all her clothes and folded them up neatly.

" 'You will bring those home,' said she, 'and bring them to your father.' Then she put on the skin.

" 'Look at yonder smooth rock,' said she. 'Come down to that rock every day and there will be fish there waiting for you. You will see me rising up in the sea and I shall call to you, but do not go out to me in case you should be drowned.' And she swam away, but before she swam away, she did sing her joy of the sea."

Ronald Iain paused and looked at me.

"She swam away," he went on, "and the children went sorrowfully back to the house. When the father was coming near to the house he saw that the cornstack was taken to pieces.

" 'Oh where is your mother?' said he, and they told him.

" 'It must have been that she saw me,' said he, 'when I was putting the skin into the heart of that stack of corn, and I am without a good woman tonight. Oh isn't it a pity that she got that skin for I was very happy when she was along with me.'

"They went home to bed and early next morning the children went down to the sea and there they found every kind of fish on the rock and their mother came and waved to them and called to them and she went on giving them fish until they grew up and prepared for marriage. Her sons and her daughters married and that is how the Clan MacCodrum came to this earth."

Ronald Iain spat toward the stove and turned to me again.

"Is that the story you heard?" he said.

"I never heard the full thing. I have heard others like it."

"You have? Well now I tell you that is how the Clan MacCodrum are called the Clan MacCodrum of the Seals, for it was on a reef that the father found the mother, and it is in North Uist that the Clan MacCodrum are, and, if they are, they are lucky. But the seals are under spells."

He got up stiffly, took a cap from the peg behind the door and a long hayfork from the corner of the stove.

"I have two beasts to feed before night," he said to me, and he went out.

"I saw the ringboats," I told Mairi. "And I spoke to Niall Mackellaig in the bar."

She nodded, went out, came back with a basin of potatoes and began to peel them.

"Were you ever in North Uist?" she said.

"No."

"It was my father's home."

"Yes, I know."

"I thought maybe it was there you heard tell of the MacCodrums."

"It was here, on this island, the last time I came."

She said nothing for a while. Her face was hidden by her long black hair as she leant over the basin on the floor.

"Old people talk strangely," she said, not looking up.

"Do you like to hear them talk?"

"Sometimes I like to hear the stories, if I haven't got a book. But it is not often my grandfather tells them. It is only when there's some old person in to see him, or a stranger like yourself, and the evenings are long when you have no book."

"Is it difficult to get books?"

"I only like Westerns and I have read them all."

"There are lots of new ones," I said.

"Did you see new ones on the mainland?"

"Yes. I'll send you some."

"I wrote to Angus for them, but he does forget."

When she had finished the potatoes, she took flour from a chest and prepared to bake bread.

"Where's your mother?" I asked.

"Is she long away?"

"She went some time before you came in."

"She does go at this hour to get the tea for Mistress Campbell, who is sick."

Mairi tossed her hair away from her eyes. "North Uist must be a backward kind of place," she said.

"I don't think so."

"Didn't you hear other stories about it? Like the one my grandfather tells?"

"Oh I see what you mean. No. When I said I'd heard stories like it, I meant in other places."

"About the MacCodrums?"

"About people who got their wives the same way. In the Faroe Islands there is a proverb—'She could no more hold herself back than the seal wife could when she found her skin.' "

"Then some of the Clan MacCodrum must have been to the Faroe Islands."

"I don't think so. It's told in Norway too, and in Iceland the man locked the—"

"Were you in Iceland?"

"No. But I have heard the story. In Iceland the man locked the sealskin in a chest and he carried the key in his pocket wherever he went, but one Sunday when he put on his Sunday suit to go to church he forgot to take the key out of the pocket of his everyday clothes. His wife had been ill and she wasn't able to go to church with him, and when he came home he could not find her. The chest was open and the sealskin gone."

"Had she any children?" said Mairi.

"Yes, and the story says she was very unhappy about leaving them. But she couldn't withstand the temptation. She put on the skin and threw herself into the sea, but before she did that she cried out and said, 'I am at a loss to know what to do. I have seven children on the land and seven children in the sea.' The children saw a great seal waiting for her as she swam away."

"Did she never come back to her husband?"

"The story says he was never as he had been, in his mind. But he had more luck fishing than before, and when he was out fishing there was often a seal swimming round his boat and there were tears in the eyes of this seal. When the children walked along the shore a seal swam along by them in the sea and cast up to them many-colored fish and beautiful shells."

By pushing her hair every minute away from her eyes and the dough, Mairi had smudged her cheeks with flour. She looked very solemn.

"Do you think does a seal really weep?" she said.

"It might be the sea-water dripping."

"My grandfather says they do weep and he says they do caress one another with kisses. They throw stones too."

"They throw stones, do they?"

"He says it is dangerous to be below them on a rocky slope."

Mairi watched me unsteadily.

"It is only what he says," she said, stifled. Covering her face with her hands, she sat down at the table. She was sobbing, inwardly, with very little sound.

When it was possible to speak again, I tried to change the subject, but she stopped me.

"It is all lies," she said. "You know well it is lies."

"What do you mean, Mairi?"

"It is well for you to come and ask about the seals. And away home with you, then, to the mainland."

"But I don't think of the stories that way—as lies or truth. I like to hear them; that's all."

She stared.

"Like reading a Western?"

"Perhaps."

"But the old people believe them."

"Well, I don't see any harm in that, do you?"

"On the mainland they wouldn't believe them."

"No."

"Not even the old people?"

"Very few of them would. But they believe lots of other things, just as strange."

"They are not backward on the mainland. Oh, I wisht I could go there to work."

"I think you should go, if you want to so much."

"My grandfather wants me to go to North Uist."

"Yes, he was telling me about the farmer there."

Unexpectedly, she laughed. "That old curmudgeon! He has whiskers on him."

The kitchen had grown dark; suddenly, it seemed to me. Mairi's mother came home with cold red hands. The wind again was whining, and when Ronald Iain came in his cap and knees and shoulders were drenched. He shook drops from the cap, but sat down to tea without changing his clothes. A smell of damp cloth and cow dung filled the room warmly.

Because of Mairi's tears, I hoped not to talk of seals again that night, but I soon knew that Ronald Iain, in his old age, not caring for the wireless and never having learned to read, finding in me an audience as attentive as any he had known long ago, had cast his mind back with new pleasure among the fragments where it usually wandered, now usually unaided and alone. After tea he took me to the inner room.

"There is something I have to show you," he said. "I did think on it while I was at the cattle."

We stooped down by his high, iron bed and between us dragged from under it a heavy chest with rusted latch and hinges. We opened it with difficulty, and breathing hard he bent and lifted layer upon layer one by one of clothes: jackets and trousers, blankets, thick woolen porridge-colored vests and underpants, old boots wrapped in yellow newspaper, empty bottles, sheep-shears carefully greased in leather sheaths, corks, buoys, some rolls of net, a rusty horseshoe. He took them up one by one in two hands, laying them deliberately on the bed or on the floor, while I stood by with a candle in my hand wondering, as toward the bottom the objects appeared more unexpected, exactly at what point of sentiment or desuetude they had been consigned to this private hoard. At last he came to a small bag, and after feeling it once or twice with both hands he took it across the room and laid it carefully on a chair. Briefly, I saw it in the candle-light, and my mind must have been filled at once with a vague memory, so that I did not hear him when he spoke to me again. When we got back into the kitchen I saw it was a sealskin purse.

"Did you ever see one like it?"

"Yes. Once. When I was a boy."

"Was it shaped like this one?"

"Almost the same, I am sure."

"Then it was an old one. They were made from the skin of the paw of the seal in my young days. And every man that had one had luck, after."

"Do you keep money in it?"

"I do. Mairi, listen, will you step over and ask Calum Angus Campbell did he bring the tobacco for me from Lochboisdale? You can tell him we have company here."

She took a mackintosh from the peg and went out saying nothing. As soon as she had gone he emptied the purse on to the table. There were a number of gold sovereigns and many half-crowns of Edward VII's reign.

"These were to be her mother's dowry," he said, "but now they are hers when she is married."

I took the purse in my hand, recalling slowly as I stroked the hair and looked at its undefined shades of fawn and black, much intimate foreboding and allusive thought until I arrived with a shock at the death of the selchie in the salmon bothy at Nairn.

I said, "It was a tobacco pouch I saw, not a purse."

"Very like. Very like."

Mairi came back with Calum Angus and a bar of cut plug. Her eyes met mine lightly as she put it on the table. She moved away at once. She was swift, direct and quiet in everything she did.

Calum Angus was a gaunt and dark man of about sixty years, more than six feet tall, with a long, narrow face, deeply lined about the mouth. His eyes were set back in hollows. He saw the purse at once and took it up.

"Man, man, it is years since I saw one of them," he said turning it this way and that.

"There is luck in them," said Ronald Iain again. He cut off a piece of tobacco and handed the bar to Calum Angus. Calum Angus sat down on the flour bin. Mairi and her mother were by the stove, the old man and I at the table.

"But there is no luck," said Ronald Iain after a long silence, "in the presence of a seal that is dead."

"I never saw a dead one, thanks be to God," said Calum Angus.

"There was many a man drowned after seeing one," said Ronald Iain.

" 'Twas the same with the mermaid."

"Is that so?" said Ronald Iain.

"It is. And she alive."

They filled their pipes. Mairi bent over her sewing, and nobody spoke till the pipes were lit.

Then Calum Angus, looking at the window, said: "It will be sixty-two years, next Lammas, since a person was drowned by a mermaid."

"Was it off Benbecula he saw her?"

"It was not. It was a party of Lochboisdale fishermen that saw her. They saw her rise up on the water near to their boat and every man of the crew threw some object at her. But the last man, when he threw what he had in his hand, she sank down. That man was drowned after. The others were safe."

Mairi's mother said, "What need was there to throw things at the creature?" Mairi did not look up.

"It is right to throw some object at a mermaid, and if she does not sink, you are safe. A knife is a very good object to throw at a mermaid."

"A knife, or anything that's made of iron," said Ronald Iain. "That will be good against a creature under spells."

There was silence again until I asked what spells the seals were under, and Ronald Iain answered.

"I do not rightly know. But I heard they were the children of the King of Lochlann, and whatever happened in the beginning I do not know, but it is given to them that their sea-longing shall be land-longing and their land-longing shall be sea-longing."

Mairi stopped sewing and looked at her grandfather.

"Where is Lochlann?" she said.

"Lochlann is the Norse lands, child. Did they teach you nothing at school?"

She glanced at me.

"And the King of Lochlann," her grandfather said, laying down his pipe against the purse, "by him came the seals and out of them came the Clan MacCodrum of the seals, in the island of North Uist; and you will be able to know one that has the blood of the seals in his body by the rock where he sits or lies, for no matter how warm the day, and his clothes being dry upon him, when he rises, there the rock will be damp where he was and the vapor from it lifting will leave crystals of sea salt beneath the sun."

Mairi looked at me for a second again, and it is by those separate seconds when our eyes met briefly that I now remember her.

THE YOUNG PEOPLE HAVE GONE FROM THE VILLAGE high up on Bolus Head in County Kerry. The whitewash is no longer on the houses. The thatch is torn and there are no children playing in the mud outside the doors. I was there in the morning early, at the end of the month of March.

When the traveling man came, with long strides shuffling down the road from the west, I was leaning on a wall that guards the village from the cliffside grass, looking at the sea quiet below me, at the three ghost islands to the south on the horizon and at the headland where the seal-killer's caves were two miles away from me across Ballinskelligs Bay. I had been there a long time gazing and was glad to be alone, but when I heard his shuffling steps I turned to look.

He was walking with a bundle on his back from the west, from the very point of Bolus Head, where the road is all uneven, and with two overcoats about him and his wide old hat he seemed to be tied up with hayrope and tin cans. His boots were greenish and half laced. His neck was bare and wrinkled, his face long and covered with gray half-inch stubble, his eyes black, their whites a bloodshot yellow, and his hand when he held it out to take what I gave him was curled like the foot of a bird. But when he spoke his voice rang clearly like a young man's voice.

"May God reward ye," he said, "and may the Holy Mary Mother

of God bring ye health and good keeping. Ye are making for the point across?" He held his long ashplant toward the seal caves. I stared at him. His lower lip hung forward and the wings of his nose looked as if they had at one time been split.

I said, "I am, but what makes you think that?"

"I know you well, sir. If you'll excuse me." He laid the ashplant on top of the wall and delved the money deep among his rags.

I said, "Did you see me in Galway or somewhere?"

"Now if ye was to be in Galway at the time of the races, it is likely I saw ye there, for I am at the races the first week of August every year, and at the latter end of March I pass by Bolus Head. For forty years I am that way, on the roads of Ireland."

"In the winter too?"

"Winter and summer, God help me. But there is no comfort in this village any more."

"A lot of the houses seem to be empty," I said.

He picked up his stick and pointed to them. "And would you believe this," he said, "I have seen it on an evening when the people were home from the fair, and ye wouldn't be able to pass by for the ass-carts that were standing and the pigs and fowl and the power of bullocks that was in it, and fine milk cows. There was not less than a family of six, young and old, to every house, I dare say."

"They have gone to the towns, I suppose."

"To America and England, some. And more of them are dead, God rest them."

We looked again across the bay. Thin sunlight came through clouds on to the water.

"I have never been to the Galway races," I said.

"It is a great meeting," he said. "There is more money passing hands in Galway that week than you'd see in Boston in a year."

As he spoke, I saw a seal far out in the water, swimming quickly away from the cliff. He held up a bony hand to shade his eyes.

"There's one o' them now for ye," he said. "They are plentiful here."

I stared at him again, trying hard to think whether I had seen him before, but his face was so unusual I felt sure I could not have forgotten it.

I said, "Where did you see me before?"

"Sure, weren't you at the seal place, beyond, two years since, yourself and Sean Sweeney the seal-killer, lying out by night above the caves?"

"Yes, I was. But were you there?"

"Look, look. There's another one. They'll be swimming over now to Sean Sweeney's. Isn't it a pity we couldn't go that way, instead of twelve miles round by the land?"

He laughed, and I found that more surprising than anything so far. He had seemed to be incapable of laughter.

"It is one of the three advices," he said. "Do ye remember them?"

"No."

"Ye must never take a short cut. That's the first advice." He became convulsed with laughter, alarmingly, plunging forward with his hands on the wall and leaning back with his upturned eyes showing yellow. Then suddenly he stopped and looked at me. "God be with ye," he said, and moved away.

"Good bye," I said. "Oh—what's your name?"

"My name is Peadar MacNamara and now I will be going."

He stood still for a minute looking at the houses. Then he crossed himself and muttered, "The blessing of God on the souls of the dead." So, with his bundle on his back he shuffled down the hill and for a long time I could hear his voice saying, as I imagined, those words again and again.

Tadhg Tracy had agreed to interpret for me as before and together that evening we went to Sean Sweeney. I asked at once about the traveling man.

"Was he as far as Bolus Head this day?" said Sean. "He'll be here tonight so. He does rest the night here once in every year."

"He wasn't here that night was he? When we were at the caves?"

"Not at all."

"Were you asking him about the seals?" said Tadhg.

"No."

"It's a wonder then you didn't."

"Does he know much?"

"He does then, and his name itself is close to what you're always asking."

"MacNamara?"

"Mac Con Mara—the son of the sea-hound. They were supposed to be descended from the seals, I think." He spoke in Irish to Sean.

Sean waved his big hands about and laughed. "He'd nearly destroy you, if you spoke of that," he said. "But I did hear it told, and the same of the O'Sullivans in County Kerry, and of the Hennessys, that their first father found their mother on the strand, and he hid her cloak away in the thatch and married her. And if she stayed with him long or short all the laughs she gave were three. The first was when a stranger came and she set the potatoes before him and he would not eat. And the second was when she saw a little girleen slip on the flagstone of the door. And the third was when she found her cloak that he had hidden. For the man of the house was one day above on the roof, putting a new thatch to it, and while he was working there above, the cloak fell down at her foot. She snatched it up and out with her to the sea."

"She was turned into a seal again," said Tadhg.

"She was, but before she swam away her man put the question to her why she had given the three laughs. Well the stranger who would not take the potatoes had lost his chance for the day."

"That's true," said Tadhg. "Never refuse food on a Monday or between two Mondays."

"And for the girleen who slipped on the flagstone, wasn't her lifting in the world of riches below the flag if she knew? There was gold buried there, do you see? And the third laugh she gave was with the cloak, for by that she knew she could go back to the sea."

Sean lit his pipe again. Tadhg was about to speak, but at that moment someone knocked at the door three times. Sean's pipe fell from his mouth to the floor. I picked it up at once, but when I went to give it to him I saw he was rigidly staring at the door. He crossed himself. He said, "The Lord have mercy on us." There was no sound outside the door.

"It will be the traveling man," said Tadhg. "That's all. It will be Peadar MacNamara, Sean."

Tadhg opened the door and it was Peadar.

"God save all here," he said. He came in and laid his bundle on the floor.

"What made you knock that way?" said Tadhg, but by now Sean Sweeney had recovered himself.

"A thousand welcomes, Peadar," said Sean, and with his ashplant between his knees Peadar MacNamara sat down as though he had only been away for an hour.

"Do you know anything about the seals?" Tadhg said when the talk of the weather and the land was at an end. "This man is gathering up the bits he can."

"I know well he is," said Peadar. "He was in the County Mayo looking for those creatures."

By now I was willing to believe that he had second sight; yet I remembered how it is with news and talk in country places. In the firelight the strange ugliness of his features was exaggerated and, remembering his laugh, I thought one might soon come to fear him for his sudden mad changes of mood. He had not removed his overcoats, nor his hat.

"The seals are a class of a fairy," he said. "That is all I know about them. They came out of the North of Ireland, from some place by the County Donegal, and the man that begat them all in the beginning was by the name of Kane."

"Well indeed, and I never heard that," said Tadhg. He repeated it in Irish so that Sean could understand. Sean nodded and pulled at his pipe.

"And, by times, they will be turned back into men," said Peadar. "As when a person stabs a knife in them, or such."

"I never remarked it," said Sean, when he understood.

"Well now, it was known long ago," Peadar said. "There was a boy from Erris stabbed a seal." He turned to me. "He was from Inish-owen in the County Donegal, not from the place in Mayo."

I nodded.

"And this boy went down to the strand to gather seaweed for the fields. He had a graip on his shoulder, for to lift the seaweed. He saw a big seal lying asleep in a hole, and went toward him. He stabbed the seal in the side with the graip, and if he did, up jumped a red-haired man! He called on the boy to stand but the boy would not do that. He ran for home and told his people what he had seen on the strand. Well, they were scolding him for what he did, but he said 'twas just a notion he got to stab the seal. That was all there was about it." With a glance at Sean Peadar stopped and repeated himself in Irish.

"Yes, yes," said Sean, absorbed.

"A year after that," said Peadar, "they went out fishing. When they were outside of Tory Island, a storm came on and they had to go into Tory and all the Tory men came down to meet them and they hauled up the boat for them. An old red-haired man came down. He was looking hard at this Erris boy. He walked up to him and stretched out his hand, and the first thing he said was, 'Don't you know me?'

" 'I don't,' said the Erris boy.

" 'Well, I know ye,' said the old man. 'Did ye ever hear tell of a man from Inishowen who stabbed a big seal with a graip, and how a big red-haired man jumped up at him?'

" 'I did,' said the boy. ' 'Twas I did it.'

" 'Well,' said the old man, 'I was the red-haired man. Come here till I show ye.'

"Well, the boy went close to him and there were three marks of a graip on his side. The boy from Erris wondered greatly."

"He would," said Tadhg, "he would."

"Nothing else would cure him, only steel," said Sean when the story had been told again in Irish.

"Well now," said Peadar, "that is what the old man said. ' 'Twas this way, it was,' he told the boy from Erris. 'I was put under a spell and my time wouldn't be over yet but for ye stabbing me with a graip that was made in a forge. Ye drew my blood,' he said, 'and I was free.'"

Peadar took off his hat and held it out toward us, laughing.

"Look at this hat will yese," he said. Sean took it in his hand and examined it this way and that.

"There's a brim on this hat," said Sean, "like the eaves of a house against the rain."

"There is indeed," said Peadar, leaning back and laughing wildly. "And it's a roof that's in need of thatching here and there. But I was to tell ye how I got that hat. 'Twas off a schoolmaster's head in Boston, Massachusetts. He gave it to me in the place of a story I told him."

"Well, well," said Tadhg, "and there's wear in it yet. Were you long in America, Peadar?"

"Ten years. And I'd go there again the morning if I had the money in my hand."

"You would come back to the roads of Ireland," said Sean, "the way you came before." He moved his great hands over the table as if to enclose the four provinces.

"Maybe I would, with the help of God," said Peadar. "For I had great wish to be in Ireland when I was over beyond."

When I said good-bye to Sean, the seal-killer, he put both his hands on mine and blessed me and asked God's blessing on the journey I had before me; then, with a glance at Peadar, he said something else in Irish and though I did not understand the words I was much moved because his hard old lips were trembling as he spoke.

I took a shirt from my knapsack and gave it to Peadar for his story. After many varied blessings, he too allowed me to leave, but at the door he said: "Remember the three advices when ye are on the road."

"Never take a short cut?" I said.

"Aye. That's the first. And never sleep in a house where an old man is married to a young woman. And never do anything in the night that you'll be sorry for at morning." He laughed and we left him there with Sean.

On the way down the hill, I asked what Sean had said.

"He said you were nearly like a traveling man yourself and he said you were young. He said there is no rest in any one of us, no matter if we are living in one place or wandering the roads, because rest is in God. Then he asked God to spare him until he might set eyes on you again, but he said it is doubtful, because he is eighty-three years of age."

That rough steamer, the *Dun Aengus*, plunged slowly westward for two hours against a head wind and came into the lee of Inishmaan, the second of the three islands of Aran which lie like a breakwater against the Atlantic about thirty miles out from Galway aslant the opening of the bay. From the rail of the steamer we could see the curraghs racing one another toward us from the shore. They bounced on the waves like long, curved leaves, shining black underneath as they rose, showing each, as it fell into the trough, the shoulders of four oarsmen pulling swiftly.

The *Dun Aengus* dropped anchor and swung about, pitching. When the first of the curraghs came alongside someone threw a rope. The Aran men caught it, drew in their oars and remained in their seats, holding on to it with one hand, rising and falling nearly six feet, I should say, against the side of the ship in the swell. The crew of the second curragh held on to the first by hand, and so with the third and fourth until they lay side by side like a pontoon bridge spanned by human arms. Then the loading began. It was surprising, when one knew that a curragh is made of tarred calico stretched on a framework of laths, to see how many great barrels of porter, sacks of flour, paraffin kegs, and such, each one could hold in that rough sea, and surprising too that it was possible to place these heavy things exactly while everything swung and tossed in an uneven rhythm. When the time came for me to step off the ship, I found that the curragh rose within reach for one moment only. If you missed that moment, you would be looking down at it many feet below.

Twenty-two head of cattle awaited the *Dun Aengus*. The sun shone suddenly between showers. A sandy beach as we drew near was splashed with red where women stood; men in close groups around each beast showed white, gray, and blue like rocks. Young girls were laughing and many children running brightly dressed. With a sling tied under its belly, a rope on its horns and ten or twelve men clinging round it, each animal was manhandled to the water's edge and with much shouting and plunging, and many backward turns, was brought through the breakers until it could no longer stand. The men went up to their necks in the water fully dressed. The other end of the rope was held by one who knelt facing the shore in the stern of a curragh and as soon as the animal was well in the water he pulled back toward it until he was near enough to take hold of its head. When he had its chin resting on the stern of the curragh, his crew began to row. So the animals were towed to the *Dun Aengus* and there slung on board. They were not allowed to swim in case they should drown in that rough sea.

Every active man, woman and child had come to the shore that day and I stayed for three hours watching their bright and lively movements. The women wore skirts of a deep red, thick and full, almost reaching their ankles. Over their heads and shoulders, the wives and widows wore big shawls, black or brown, but the children, and the girls who were not yet married, had bright scarves of many-colored threads, crossed over their breast and under their arms and tied with a knot at the back. The men's trousers are woven at home out of wool, undyed in the weft and blue in the warp, which gives them a shadowy worn appearance. The fly buttons are not covered and the narrow trouser legs are split at the ankles, like cuffs. They wear heavy jerseys, gray or blue, knitted in an intricate pattern, and a sleeveless tweed waistcoat. Some have a blue serge jerkin and some still wear the bawneen—an undyed jerkin almost white, for which they were so famous long ago. On their feet they wear pampooties—flat-soled shoes of uncured cowhide with the hair outside like the rivlins of the North. These grow hard and stiff if a man walks on dry land too long, but as the Aran Islander spends half his life in the sea, there is little danger of that.

When the evening came we went to the public house. The men who had been loading the cattle came in two's and three's and sat on benches and barrels against the walls, and the seawater from their clothes settled in small pools on the stone floor. In the middle of the floor stood a bucket full of Guinness, and when everyone had arrived and found somewhere to sit, it was ladled out in mugs by one who stood in the center. There were only two mugs for the whole company. Each took his time to drink and passed it back when it was empty to be filled again for his neighbor.

The man in charge of the bucket was the first to speak to me and I found to my relief and pleasure that he knew quite a lot of English. His name was Mourteen. He saw me at the counter examining my map. He filled the two mugs and gave them out. Then he came and stood beside me.

"That will be Galway City," he said, pointing.

"Yes. That's it."

"It is a great map you have. There's the Claddagh marked there. I never saw a map marked with the Claddagh."

He called another man to him and pointed to the old foreshore of Galway where the fishing-people live. He explained, in Irish, what the map meant but the other man seemed unable to understand.

"You go where you go with this map," said the man in charge of the bucket, searching in his mind for English words.

"I don't often look at it," I told him. "But when I am among islands, I like to know exactly where I am."

"And will it mark this island—Inishmaan?"

"Here it is. Look."

He called two others up to him and they looked, and for some minutes the whole company was round me looking at the map.

"It has Carraroe marked here," said the man with the bucket.

"What is Carraroe?" I asked, but he left me to ladle out more drink. The others sat down again and the place grew dark.

"I'll show you Carraroe," he said, and in Irish he asked the land-lord for a candle. When the candle came, I looked about me and saw the shadows of unusual faces, wild strands of hair and out-stretched arms, fantastic in their shapes upon the white-washed wall; also a glistening dampness where the water gathered on the floor.

"Carraroe," said the man with the bucket, "is the nearest on the Connemara coast to us. What we cannot bring to Galway with the steamer, we will bring by curragh into Carraroe. And if you will excuse me asking you, is it here for bits of the rock you are?"

"No. But . . . bits of the rock?"

"There is no harm in it," he said. "There is a lot of men come here with maps and they studying the kind of rock we have on the island and taking pieces with them when they go away."

"Oh yes, I understand. No, I am not studying that."

"And there's them that look at birds," he said.

"Yes. But not me. I look at seals when I can."

"At what, if you'll excuse me?"

"At the seal—at the Rón Mór."

"Oh, her! Well she's plentiful about these islands and about the coast across."

"Does she breed here?"

"I don't know does she breed." He turned to the others, spoke in Irish and filled the mugs again.

"That's right," he said when he came back, "You have no Irish, have you?"

"No."

"They tell me it is under the cliffs of Moher the Rón Mór does breed in autumn, but to the north you'll see her in the summertime, and if you see one you'll see a hundred lying on the rocks at low tide. They did use to hunt them in the old days there. But now they have the place to themselves." He looked at the map again and pointed to the coast of Connemara. "There now," he said. "Out from Mween-ish that's a great place for seals. Oh, by God, by God, this map is great." He called the others round us again. "I am telling them," he said, "how you have the Skerd Rocks marked on your map—every one. And that is the most dangerous place a man can pass through, for it is one mass of sunken islands at high tide."

"That's where the seals lie, do they?" I said, pointing.

"They do, at low tide you will see plenty of them there."

A tall old man, leaning over me shook his head and spoke.

"He says the Connemara men used to be out on the Skerd Rocks killing seals. But not on the Black Ledge, he says."

"Why not on the Black Ledge?"

"He says you have your finger on the Black Ledge now. He says the kind the Black Ledge is, it is a rock that is under water with a high tide or a stormy sea."

"And there are no seals on it?"

"No seals on it."

"But on the other rocks there are seals?"

"He says he passed Black Ledge a hundred times and there were no seals on it. It is with the curragh he passed it."

The bucket was filled again, foaming brown and white, and was put back on the middle of the floor. The tall old man went on talking. Despairing of the subject of the Black Ledge, I tried my three words of Irish, but he talked still more and faster. The man in charge of the bucket came back to us, and consulted the landlord, with a nod at me.

"He is asking are you one of the Fishery men?"

"No, no," I said, trying to think of an acceptable description. "I am just going about—on a sort of a holiday."

"Is it the big sharks you look to and the seals?" said the man with the bucket.

"The right English for what he is asking," said the landlord, "is this word naturalist."

"No. I'm just on a holiday."

"The woman of the house has English," said the man with the bucket. "You will come home with me. She has plenty of English for the two of us."

Several men made ready to leave. As they stood up I noticed the dark marks left on the benches by their damp trousers. The tall man came with us. There was no rain now and under a great moon the walls so near together enclosing tiny fields made one gray hill of stone, as I looked up, but below the road toward the sea I could see the silvery grass between the walls, and the straight lazybeds, black, now sown with potatoes. Scattered houses shone whitely.

"Every bit of land there is land that is made," said Mourteen when he saw me looking at it. The language problem made me decide not to question him, but he explained himself. "It is the men of this island that carried sand from the shore and laid it on the rock and carried seaweed. That is how the land was made."

"It was all bare rock?"

"Bare rock."

When we came round the edge of the hill, we saw acres and acres of bare rock ahead of us, a desert of flat gray shelves. His was the last of the houses.

"Those gardens there are my gardens. I have them sown with Up-to-Dates. The most of the people sow Up-to-Dates. They are more of a floury potato I think."

We went in. Mourteen's wife was a middle-aged woman, large and strong in her body, her face full of life, with bright eyes, her skin like a young girl's. She was dancing a baby boy, her grandchild, on her knee, his long white dress draped on her skirt of red, and beside her, deep in the fireplace with her back against the chimney, a little girl sat looking out at us, her face like a lively pool in the shadows.

Mourteen's wife greeted me in English. "The journey was cruel today with the *Dun Aengus* surely. Did they take the cattle on at Inisheer?"

"No. It was too rough."

"There now! Isn't that the misfortune for the people of that island with another week of feeding to be lost on the cattle and it nearly into the month of May. You were lucky so, Mourteen."

"We were in the same case," said Patsy, her son, "only for the wind lying in the back of this island."

"I am not blaming God," she said to me, "but my son Patsy was two days lost at sea, it isn't three weeks since, himself and the crew of two curraghs—astray in the fog they were, and astray from one another, and one curragh came in on the coast of Connemara and he on the coast of Clare. They weren't able to rise from the curragh, with the cold, when they came ashore."

"Had you any food and drink?" I said to Patsy.

"We did chew dulse."

"Well there's little food in that," said his mother.

"It is good against the thirst."

We had tea, and the tall old man whose name I now knew to be Josie Coneely spoke at length. Mourteen's wife turned to me when he came to an end.

"He has been trying to tell you," she said, "how you'll not see any seals on the Black Ledge. Is it seals you want to see?"

"Yes, we were talking about them."

"Well, he says it is how there was an O'Malley man out of Mweenish, Edward O'Malley, and he was without company in the house, only himself and his wife and little daughter." She looked at her grandchild in the fireplace as she spoke.

"It was not a right daughter," said Mourteen.

"It was a little girl he found in the mountains and took her and reared her at home with his wife. That's why I do call her his daughter. Now this O'Malley man was out on the Skerd Rocks and he killed nine seals there that day, and his wife was afraid for him and she said to the little girl how she thought it was a long time he was away. 'He is out now at the Black Ledge,' says this little one to her, 'and he has killed nine seals there, but for ever again no one will see a seal on that rock.'"

"She had knowledge," said Mourteen.

A small boy ran into the room, pulled Josie Coneely by the hand and spoke as though he had just seen a house on fire. Josie left with him, and he seemed amused.

"His cow is calving," said Mourteen's wife. "What took him to be talking of the seals?" she said when he had gone.

I told her how it had started with me.

"Well you chose the right man, when you spoke to a Coneely!"

This made everybody laugh, especially Patsy.

"I have seen the Connemara men fight like dogs for less than that," he said.

"There was a woman in this island itself," his mother said. "Nora was her name and she was cutting one of them, cutting a seal up, for to get the oil—there's a cure in seal oil—and she cut her hand so badly it was very sore by her, and myself went to see her and I was asked by the woman of the house where I was lodging. 'How is Nora?' she says.

" 'The hand is sore by her,' I said.

" 'Oh, 'tis hard to cure her,' says she back to me. 'For those seals are some of the Coneely's who were put under magic. They were cursed or something,' says she, 'and turned into seals.' "

"That's how the fight began," said Patsy. "One said to a Coneely man in a kind of a joke—'I saw a Coneely swimming by the curragh,' says he. Well there was murder then between himself and the Coneely's in the pub."

Mourteen said, "It is how the old people told that one of those Coneely men of Connemara took a seal-woman for his wife. That's how it started. None of that family ever ate the meat of a seal."

" 'Twouldn't be natural if he did," said Mourteen's wife and nobody laughed any more.

At odd moments as we talked, young men had come into the room, singly or in two's, with a quiet greeting and there were now six or seven of them sitting haphazard wherever they found space.

"Did you ever hear it told," I said to Mourteen, after a long silence, "how the seals came to be in the beginning?"

"What way is it you mean?" he said puzzled.

"A traveling man told me that they were supposed to start with one called Kane."

"They are great ones to tell a story, those traveling men," said Mourteen.

"And in the Orkney Islands, they told me that the seals were supposed to be the souls of drowned men."

"God save us," said Mourteen's wife, and I did not know whether she was shocked or amused.

"Well now," said Mourteen, thinking like one trying to remember the words of a song long forgotten. "I did hear of the souls of the drowned living under the sea long ago. But it wasn't seals they were. I think it wasn't seals."

"You are thinking now of your father's story, God have mercy on his soul," said Mourteen's wife. "You are thinking of the axe and the hook."

"The axe and the hook and the knife," said Mourteen. "I wonder have I it yet?"

"You have of course. You often told it."

Mourteen was quiet for several minutes and I saw he was whispering words to himself. What he then said, in Irish, was translated to me later.

"Well now," he said, "I think I have, but if I have it wrong it is because it is long since I told it." He whispered again and began.

"There was one night a man going fishing out from the Claddagh in Galway. This man was going out with his three sons, and they had no one else for a crew. They were waiting a long time on the others. The old man didn't know what he should do; he hadn't enough help to go to sea. 'Twasn't long till he saw a man making toward him on the strand, and he riding a white horse. He shouted to the sons that there was a stranger coming riding and that he didn't know who he was. The horseman came as far as them and spoke and asked were they going fishing or where were they going. The boatman said they were going fishing.

" 'You are a stranger here,' says he. 'I don't know you. Who are you?'

" 'Yes, indeed, I'm a stranger,' says the man of the white horse, 'and if ye are going to sea tonight, take with ye three things: an axe, a hook and a knife.'

"When he had said that and they turned around, the man of the white horse had disappeared.

" 'Why do ye think he said that to us?' asked the old man, of his sons.

" 'I don't know,' says one of them. 'But what harm can it do to us to take them with us till we see?'

"One of the sons went to the house and brought with him an axe, a hook and a knife. They had their nets boarded and they shoved out the boat and went to sea. There were a lot of other boats out before them. The night was very calm. But before long there came a great squall of wind. The old man said that it was time to be pulling for the land, that he was afraid the night was going to harden, for the sky was bad-looking and the sooner they made shore the better.

" 'We may as well pull for home,' says the sons, 'as we haven't the help.'

"They started to row and they weren't long rowing when the sea rose, and they saw the mighty wave coming toward them.

" 'This will put us to the bottom, 'tis so big,' shouted one of the sons. 'The boat will not carry it.'

" 'Throw out the hook, see will it be any help,' says the old man. 'We may as well take the stranger's advice.'

"When the wave was almost on top of them the son threw out the hook. The wave split in two and passed on either side of them without doing any damage. They battled on and battled on as well as they were able—and strong men they were—and soon they saw the second wave coming, as high as a hill.

" 'Heave out the axe!' shouted the father.

"One of the sons threw it out and the minute he did the wave split in two at either side of the boat and did no harm. They pulled on another while—getting bad the night was with gale and heavy rain. They didn't know what to do—'twas so dark that they couldn't see where they were going. On came another wave, as high as a hill, and they were sure that this would finish them.

" 'Throw out the knife!' says the old man.

"One of the sons threw it out, and the wave split in two and passed on either side with a sweep that threw the boat up on the strand. They were safe. Whatever way one of the men looked around, he saw an oar being washed in, and a piece of a boat.

" 'There has been a drowning for sure,' says the father.

"The wind was so high and the night so bad that they weren't able to shove the boat up for a while, but they got it up a little and tied it

with a big pelt of a rope and filled the boat with stones. They made
for home, and the gale was taking the corn-stooks and stacks. It was
a good while later before it got calmer. They ate their supper when
they got home—'twas very late then—and then they heard someone at the door.

" 'Who's there?' the old man shouted.

" 'Open!' shouts the person outside. 'I want to go in.'

"One of the sons opened the door, and who should be there but
the man of the white horse.

" 'Are your sons asleep?' says he.

" 'No,' says the old man.

" 'Tell them come out—I want them,' says the horseman.

"The three sons went outside the door.

" 'Jump up here on the horse, men,' says he.

" 'There's not room,' says one of them.

" 'There will be,' says the horseman. 'I'll walk, and the horse can
take ye all.'

"They mounted the horse and set off, the stranger walking and
they riding, and didn't feel until they were in a big town. They were
terrified when they didn't know where they were; they saw big
crowds of people, men and women coming from a dance, and they
up and down the street together, holding one another, and having
great sport and pastime.

" 'Now,' says the horseman, 'don't take any notice of them. Come
along with me to the top of the street. There's a big house there—
that's where we're going. When ye go in, don't speak a word or
answer any question till ye come out to me again.'

"He reached the door, and it was opened by a man that was
standing inside.

" 'In ye go now, boys,' says the horseman. 'Ye are needed inside.'
They went in.

" 'Go you up to the top room,' says the doorman to the eldest son.
'There's somebody waiting there for you.'

"He went up to the room, and when he opened the door he saw
a parlor the like of which he had never seen before, 'twas so fine and

well done up. When he looked around what should he see but a young woman stretched on a bed, a woman so beautiful that he had never seen her like with the light of his two eyes before. Stuck in her forehead was the axe!"

The little girl gasped and I looked to the back of the chimney where she was by the fire.

" 'Come over here,' says the young woman, 'and pull the axe out of my forehead. That's your handiwork tonight.'

"He pulled out the axe, and came down to the kitchen without saying a word.

"The doorman then spoke to the second son. 'Now 'tis your turn to go up to the room,' says he. 'You're needed there.'

"He went up and what should he see but a woman stretched on a bed there and the hook stuck in her shoulder.

" 'Come over here,' says she, 'and pull out this hook. This is the result of your handiwork tonight.'

"He pulled it out, and pretended not to hear what she was saying, and when he had it pulled she sat up in the bed and looked at him for a while, and when he thought she was looking at him too much he walked off down into the kitchen. The two brothers were there waiting for him. The doorman then spoke to the youngest brother.

" 'Your turn to go up now,' says he.

"Up he went and he saw the most beautiful queen he ever saw in his life, before or after, and a knife stuck in her head behind her ear.

" 'Come over here,' says she, 'and pull out this knife. My blessing on you and my curse on those who have given you orders. There isn't a young woman in the town tonight, except the three of us, who hasn't got a husband. We're three sisters. My curse on the man of the white horse. Only for him we would have got the three of ye tonight. He's outside waiting for ye now, but we'll have our revenge on him.'

"He left the room and the three of them went out to the man of the white horse where he was waiting for them.

" 'Up on the horse with ye now,' says he, 'and don't ye speak for ever again about what ye have seen or heard tonight. Don't ever again go to sea—if ye do, I don't want to say what may happen to ye.'

"The three mounted the white horse and weren't long on their journey till they reached home again. Yet the journey back took them seven times longer than the journey there.

" 'Go in home now,' says the man of the white horse, 'and I forbid ye ever again to go on the sea. If ye do ye will be taken by the women of the host. There were thirty-one men drowned tonight and ye saw them up and down the street with their women. 'Tisn't how they were drowned but taken away. I'm leaving ye now,' he said, 'and ye won't see me any more. Only for me ye would be where ye'er comrades are.'

"That is my story," said Mourteen.

The little girl came out of the fireplace and clambered on his knee asking questions. The young men blessed his household for the night and went their way; Patsy and his wife prepared to leave the room with the baby, long since asleep; and Mourteen's wife stooped in her red dress over the fire. The little girl slipped from Mourteen's knee, not waiting for an answer. She pulled her grandmother aside and knelt beside the fire. She took away the larger pieces of turf and gathered the red cinders into a little heap. She raked the sandy-colored ashes over this and pressed them down with her hands. Then she drew a cross upon them and spoke her prayer.

"What was she saying?" I asked when she had finished.

"In English, is it? She did say: 'We rake this fire as the pure Christ rakes all. Mary at its foot and Brigid at its top. The eight highest angels in the City of Graces preserving this house and the people till day.' "

One afternoon, in the summer, I went for the last time to the "Village of the Love of God." I opened the door of the ferry house and saw that the fire was red, but very low and silent. Nets, oars and a disused buoy lay in the rafters as before. The room smelt of tar and turf smoke and a bumblebee was in a frenzy against the window in the still heat of June. There was no one about. I sat on the table lazily wondering where Michael the Ferry would be. His boat was at the door. I went out to look at it. Then I walked to the end of the quay and sat on the hot stone.

It was one of those days of heat, rare in Ireland, when a haze hangs over the sea and hill like a blue veil, trembling slightly. I heard a lark, high up, and a scythe-stone ringing. The waves slapped the quayside gently underneath my feet, and far out moving from the open sea a familiar black head appeared, then another; both went down and drawing nearer showed themselves again. The tide had just turned and they were swimming with it up the sound.

I watched the houses opposite, across the ferry, for some sign of life, but nothing moved there except thin smoke from chimneys rising straight, and my eyes wandered southward along the shore, where I had walked with Michael on my last day here, to the Beach of the Seals below the green graveyard. The yellow sand was dazzling even at this distance and it seemed quite deserted. I decided to swim over and lie down there in the sun. And so I began to take off my clothes.

I pulled my shirt over my head and looked at the beach again, my arms still in the sleeves, my mind in a dream, and now I could see a black object on the sand very near to where the waves were breaking. I watched it steadily, imagining it to be a seal asleep as they so often sleep just out of reach of the water, but a moment later it moved and was divided into two parts. A shout came from it and I saw that it was two men. They had been kneeling on the sand and now stood up. One of them waved his arms and I thought he was beckoning to me. I waved with my shirt and began to take off my shoes, but he shouted again and again until I realised that he wanted something urgently. At last I heard what he said. It was "the boat!"

I went to fetch the oars. They were lying in their old place by the wall of Michael's house. I threw them into the boat as I had seen him do, climbed down the steps of the quay and shoved off. When I looked over my shoulder at the Beach of the Seals, I saw that the two men were crouching down again. I was puzzled and afraid and I rowed as fast as I could, clumsily tearing my knuckles as I handled the heavy sea oars. I had seen that the tide was running in, so I made straight for the middle of the sound and moved fast in its stream. The two seals caught up with me as I rowed. I watched them and did not look again over my shoulder to the beach. Sometimes they swam slowly on their backs, keeping level with the boat just below the surface of the water, their front flippers lying easily on their chests, their hind ones paddling without effort; then one would turn, put his head up for breath, and with a splash and a twist of his lithe body, using all four flippers in a kind of breast stroke, plunge and chase the other with such power that he set up a wash like a fast boat. It was a game. It was a mock fight once when they rose to the surface together biting each other's mouths, growling a growl that changed halfway into a childlike squall. Then they would separate and dive or float near the surface again. They moved in the water with grace and enjoyment.

Though I watched them with enjoyment, I knew there was something wrong on the Beach of the Seals. When I came near and turned the bows of the ferry boat on to it I saw that both the men were Cregans. The old one, Patrick Sean, whom I had thought of, on my other visit, as "the man in the corner," was up to his thighs in the water waiting to pull me ashore. I jumped out and we pulled the boat up together without speaking. The young man, Joseph Tom Cregan, now about twenty years old, was kneeling on the sand nearby, his knees astride the body of a child all limp and white, his hands on her back pressing firmly and relaxing by turns.

"I don't know am I doing this right," he said to me without stopping.

"Have you sent for a doctor?"

"Mickeen ran above to the shop with the telephone. But he's away long and I'm afraid there's neither priest nor doctor at their homes."

"She'll have little comfort in either now, God rest her and have mercy," said Patrick Sean.

"There is breath in her yet."

He had pulled her wet clothes off and they lay brightly colored in a heap, but there was still a red ribbon round her neck. I loosened it. He had put his own jacket under her head and the old man's about her waist and legs.

The old man prayed; not for her life, I knew, but for her soul.

I saw that the red ribbon held a crucifix now half buried in the sand, and I wished I had not taken it from her neck, for, though we could hear a whisper of breath each time he pressed her ribs, and could see her neat white shoulders moving with the movement of his hands, I felt sure she had been dead for some time. Her long hair, very black, clung to her skin in wisps, sticky with salt water, and her face turned sideways on the jacket was discolored like a bruise.

The doctor and the priest arrived together with Mickeen. The doctor felt her pulse. "She'll be all right," he said. He gave her an injection, and when at last her breath came regularly without help he told us we could move her. Joseph Tom Cregan washed the sand from the crucifix and tied it again to her neck. Wrapping the jackets round her, we took her to the ferry boat and there she lay in the doctor's arms as he sat in the stern. The Cregans rowed. Mickeen and I sat together in the bows. Mickeen looked ill. He did not speak.

In the ferry house that evening it was difficult to tell how deeply Mickeen was affected by the accident. He told his father how it happened. Paddling some distance from him at low tide she had fallen over a rock and had been dragged down. She had never learned to swim. It was ten or fifteen minutes before he thought of looking for her and then he saw her rolling where the waves broke. He pulled her out himself. Michael the Ferry said nothing.

"Whose child is she?" I asked him.

"She is Peggy Ann Moloney's child, God bless her."

"Is it Brigid Ann?" said Mickeen's younger brother, with his mouth full and his face daubed with jam.

"Now take a sup o' the buttermilk," said Michael the Ferry, "and don't be choking yourself the way you did o' Tuesday."

"Is it Brigid Ann is coming, Da?" said Mickeen's sister, younger still.

"Now don't be talking with your tea, the crowd o' ye."

"I want an egg with spots on, Da!"

"Sure, didn't she bring ye plover's eggs last evening, child."

"They're gone again. We lost them."

"The Lord save us," said Michael the Ferry, but he took some plover's eggs from the mantelpiece where they were hidden and put them on the table.

"She is that way, Brigid Ann," he said to me, "finding every nest on the bog and gathering shells from the shore. She is weak, the poor girl, and she'll speak no harm to anyone. She is very quiet and happy in herself but if a person sent her for a pound of sugar it might be a packet of candles she'd bring home. That kind of way she is, God bless her."

"The old man could have saved her sooner if he wanted," Mickeen said.

"What's that you say, Mickeen?"

"Patrick Sean Cregan saw her before me."

"Why do you say that?"

"I know well he did."

"Well. Well," said Michael the Ferry and he put a hand to his forehead.

"And he lifted no hand to help me when I was with her in the water."

"Now, Mickeen," said Michael. "Patrick Sean Cregan is a great age and he will be here with us presently and we'll not speak more of this to him, you nor me."

"All right so. But there's no word of a lie in that."

"Now Mickeen, I'll tell ye," his father said, worried. "Some of the old people have ways that you and I think strange. In my father's day, a man might be drowning in the sound close by the door here and no man stir to put the boat out to him. What the sea will take, the sea must take—that's what my father would say. And there was many a story told in those days of men being saved that were innocent in their lives to the day they were taken from the sea, but turned wicked after, and robbed and sometimes went to murder the hand that saved them. Now Patrick Sean Cregan is a great age," said Michael the Ferry.

They unfolded the settle bed and the children climbed in for the night.

Patrick Sean Cregan knocked once on the door with the head of his ashplant and came in and sat by the fire. I asked him when the chance came about MacNamara, the travelling man. His face lit up with recognition.

"A great one to bring news," he said.

"I met him in County Kerry."

"Sure there's no place in Ireland that he doesn't travel in the year, and there's hardly a man in Ireland he doesn't know."

"Has he got what you'd call 'the knowledge'?"

"I don't know, then, I don't know. A lot of those traveling men have it. And more would like you to think they have it, I do believe. But I'll tell you this, 'tis no word of a lie, 'twas he told me never leave a cow on Michael Martin's strand, and she strayed down there calving and I lost her."

I wondered whether it was the sight of me that made him remember the loss of his Jersey cow, or whether, in his old age, he thought of it most of the time.

"Peadar MacNamara was talking of a family called Kane," I said.

"Were you asking him about the seals?" said Patrick Sean.

"Yes."

"The seals are called Kanes by some," said Michael the Ferry.

"Well, there was a cow that calved on Michael Martin's strand, and the calf she had was a seal. He could have told you that. He does know a great number of things about the sea. And one of those Kanes had charge of the cow Glas Ghaibhne. Was it that he was telling you about the Kanes?"

"No. He didn't say much."

"It's a wonder he didn't," said Patrick Sean.

"Those Kanes are from this part of Mayo," said Michael the Ferry.

"They are," said Patrick Sean, "and it's here they were in the beginning and it is by them the seals came here."

He looked at me. He laid his ashplant across his knees and began to speak very fast.

He said: "Long ago and a long time ago it was; if I was there then I wouldn't be here now, or if I were, I'd have a new story or an old story, or maybe I wouldn't have any story at all. Even if I were to lose only the back teeth or the front teeth or the teeth farthest back in my head—there was three brothers of the Kanes. And there was a smith in Ireland and he had a cow named Glas Ghaibhne. She had as much milk as twenty cows, but there had to be a man watching her from morning to sunset because she was under a spell. Any man who would guard her from morning to sunset would be given a sword for his pay. But it took a good man to guard her, for every day that she was feeding she would travel sixty miles, eating a good bite here and a good bite there, and going hither and over, and wherever she went he must never go before her, nor hold her, nor stand in her way, but follow her always, thirty mile outward and thirty mile homeward the day she walked least. She was the best cow that ever was in Ireland before or since. Well, there was a young fellow of the Kanes there and, 'I'll guard her,' says he. So he guarded the cow till night and the smith gave him a sword. His brother was as good a man as he and he went the next day and guarded her till night and the smith gave him a sword. 'I'm as good a man as ye,' says the youngest brother, but when he went to guard her he slipped his foot and in a moment the cow was gone.

" 'Now,' said the smith, 'I'll give you a year and a day to find the cow Glas Ghaibhne.'

"The three brothers set out in their ship and sailed over the sea till they came to a strand like the one below the house here, very far from home. There was a man on the strand and he building a fence to keep out the sea.

" 'Well,' says the youngest of the brothers Kane, 'That's a foolish work you're at.'

" 'It's not a bit more foolish than what you're at,' says the man. 'I am under a spell by the man that took the cow. The name of that man is Balor Beimeann, and he has one eye in the middle of his forehead. And if you want to get the cow you must eat seven years' butter with three sorrel leaves and seven years' meat. You must lie with three hundred dark-haired women and three hundred red-haired women and three hundred fair-haired women, and have children by them in nine months' time.'

" 'That's a terrible number of children,' says Kane.

" 'Well,' says the man who was building the fence, 'those nine hundred women are the guardians of Balor Beimeann's daughter up there on the hill. He doesn't let anyone visit her, but if you can at all you must go to her, for no one will ever kill Balor except the son of his daughter, and 'tis only by Balor's death that I will ever be free.'

" 'Very well,' says Kane to him. 'I'll go to Balor's daughter, if I can. But never mind these other women,' says he.

" 'You will go first to Balor's daughter,' says the man. 'She will be pleased with you and like you. But you must treat all these other women the same way or they'll tell Balor that they saw you there. Don't worry,' says he. 'I'll give you a belt to wear and you'll be as good after the last woman as after the first. Bring all these children to me.'

"Kane stayed on this island for the nine months until each of the women had a child, and the daughter of Balor on the hill had a son. He brought the children to the man on the strand; found him there still making his fence. Very well, when he brought them to the strand, the son of Balor's daughter surpassed all the children in strength.

" 'Take him home with you,' says the man on the strand. 'When you go out with the children into the deep sea, throw the whole lot of them out but keep the daughter's son. His name will be Lui of the Long Arm and 'tis he will kill his grandfather Balor Beimeann.'

"When Kane took the children out into the deep sea, he opened his cloak and every one of them fell into the sea. And they were turned into a school of seals. So that's how the seals came to be." Patrick Sean looked at Michael the Ferry.

"It is, of course," said Michael.

Patrick Sean looked at me, and went on.

"Kane took the son of Balor's daughter home, but he was not thriving. So didn't he take a ship again, himself with the child, and brought him to the man on the strand. There he was still at work with the fence. 'This child is not thriving,' says Kane.

" 'Is that so?' says the man on the strand. 'Oh, I see that,' says he.

'Take him up to Balor, on the hill,' he says. 'The child will not thrive till his grandfather calls him by name.'

"So Kane went to Balor and asked him for work.

" 'What can you do?' says Balor.

" 'I am the best gardener in the world,' says Kane.

" 'I have a better gardener than you,' says Balor.

" 'You have not,' says Kane. 'What can your gardener do?'

" 'The tree that he plants on Monday morning has the finest ripe apples on Saturday night.'

" 'That's nothing,' says Kane to him. 'The tree that I plant in the morning, I'll pick apples from it in the evening; every one of them the finest and ripest that ever you saw.'

" 'What child is that with you?' said Balor.

" 'My own child. His mother is dead.'

" 'I don't like children near my castle,' said Balor. 'But if you are such a gardener as you say, then I will keep you for a time. But what wages would you be looking for?' says he.

" 'I want no wages,' says Kane, 'only the cow Glas Ghaibhne to be given to me when my time is up.'

" 'In a year and a day you'll get her,' says Balor.

"Balor spoke no word to the child until one day Kane stumbled on the step of the door, and he with an armful of apples. All the people went to gather them up, and the son of Balor's daughter surpassed every one of them in his swiftness, and Balor let a shout out of him then. 'Take away with you that little Long Arm,' he said.

" 'Oh, he has his name now,' said Kane, and after that the child began to thrive.

"When he had his time worked, Kane went to ask Balor for the cow.

" 'Certainly,' says Balor. 'But I must tell you,' says he, 'there is only one way I can give her to you, for it is my daughter has her halter, and whatever man she chooses to throw the halter to, it is only he that can have the cow.'

"So Kane and Balor stood below the daughter's window, and she saw it was Kane that was there. She threw the halter to Kane.

"Balor let a shout out of him again. 'How could you do that, my daughter?' said he.

" 'Oh, Father,' said she, 'there's a crooked cast in every woman's hand. I did intend to throw it to you.'

"Very well, Kane got the cow and he brought her and the child back to Ireland to the smith.

"When Balor Beimeann heard that the child that was in Ireland was his own daughter's child, over he came to destroy all Ireland. He had an eye in the middle of his forehead which he kept covered always with nine shields of thick leather so that he might not open his eye and turn it on anything, for no matter what Balor looked on he burned it to ashes. When he came to Ireland, all that he saw was the tops of the wild iris and the tops of the rushes, and these are burned red ever since, but before he could see more, Lui of the Long Arm, his daughter's son, put a spear into his eye and killed him.

"Balor said then, 'Let me rest my head on your body and I shall leave you a virtue.' But Lui suspected him. He got a big stone and put Balor's head on that. A tear fell from Balor Beimeann's eye on to the stone and it split the stone in two. That is my story," said Patrick Sean Cregan, and his voice gathered speed to end as he had begun in a gabbled monotone, "God to my lips! Death will come. Great the tidings! The blessing of God on the souls of the dead!"

Mickeen's small brother had started crying halfway through the story and, relenting at last, Michael lifted him on to his knee, singing over and over again

> "We are twelve tinkers so airy and free,
>   So airy and free, so airy and free,
>   Seeking for one of thy daughters from thee"

until the child was quiet.

"God bless him," said Patrick Sean Cregan.

"And thanks be to God," said Michael the Ferry, "that Peggy Ann Moloney has her child safe this night."

"Thanks be to God," said Patrick Sean. "But I would say that's not the end of it." The room seemed very silent.

"God bless us all," said Michael.

"Now, I will not turn it to God," said Patrick Sean Cregan, "and may all be safe where it is told, but last night there was three knocks at my door and when I went to open it there was no person there. No one at all."

"Lord save us," said Michael. The child was asleep in his arms.

Patrick Sean Cregan pointed at me with his stick.

"This man made good speed coming over with the boat today," he said.

"Ye found her awkward, I doubt," said Michael the Ferry.

"A bit heavy." I told him how the two seals had followed me all the way.

"They do like to follow the ferry boat," he said. "There were full sixty, one time at a funeral. My father told me of it, for it was at his father's funeral they were. Like every man o' the ferry he had great regard for those creatures, and when his coffin was resting on the quay here, and the mourners keening by it, didn't the seals gather in the water one by one. The mourners laid the coffin in the stern o' the boat, laid it there with the head to the west and the feet to the east, and they rowed along and over to the graveyard. And if they rowed, the seals came after in a single line. I remember my father saying there was one long line of heads above the water as far as you could see. And when they came to the Beach of the Seals and landed the coffin there, the seals came out of the water and were there on that beach, and they keening and lamenting all together till the funeral was done."

Michael the Ferry carried the small boy back to bed. He started crying again.

"Be quiet, will ye?" said Michael.

"Sing me another."

"I will not. Ye'll go asleep now—that's the boy."

"Sing me one more and then I'll go asleep."

Mickeen shouted, "Tell him what the cat says," and began to squall like a cat.

"I will not then. 'Tis too noisy. And you, Mickeen, be quiet."

Patrick Sean Cregan rose stiffly from his chair and said "good night" to Michael. Because I had to leave early next morning I shook him by the hand and said "good bye." He took his hand from mine and touched my cheek.

"Ye have grown stouter since I saw ye last," he said. He ran his fingers lightly round my chin and upon my forehead. "May the Lord bring ye safely from the next twelve months and not weaken ye," he said. "May the evil eye of a person never see ye. May ye be seven times better a year from tonight, and when ye come again may there be no more straws in the thatch than there are welcomes for ye."

Mickeen's small brother let out a scream.

"One more!"

"Then what does the skylark say?" said Michael the Ferry, bending over the child, who grew quiet at once. "She says, 'Who robbed my nest? If it is a large person with sense and wisdom, may God take him away. If it is an innocent little being, may God leave him to his own mother.'"

The Music of the Seals

The seals are very fond of music. Everywhere I went people told me that, but I was never fortunate enough to hear at first hand the music that belongs to them. I believe there is much that remains privately in the minds of the country people of the West, but can only give here a few pieces that have found their way into print. I shall put first a ballad, "The Grey Selchie of Sule Skerrie," and, last, a few notes which were sung by a seal off the island of Skomer, Pembroke-shire, in 1946, and recorded there by Dr. Ludwig Koch. These two have moved me more than the others.

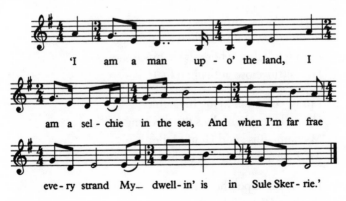

'I am a man up - o' the land, I am a sel - chie in the sea, And when I'm far frae eve - ry strand My— dwell - in' is in Sule Sker - rie.'

The Sule Skerry is a rock in the Atlantic about fifty miles south-west of Orkney. Within living memory it was frequented by large numbers of seals. Some of the verses of the ballad are still remembered in the islands of Orkney and Shetland, but the tune was very nearly lost. It was first noted down in 1938 by Dr. Otto Andersson, who heard it sung by Mr. John Sinclair on the island of Flotta, Orkney. In his article "Väinämöinen och Vellamos Jungfru" (Budkavlen, Åbo, 1947) Dr. Andersson says: "I had no idea at the time that I was the first person to write down the tune. The pure pentatonic form of it and the beautiful melodic line showed me that it was a very ancient melody that I had set on paper." A full version of the words was sent to Dr. Andersson by Miss Annie G. Gilchrist.

The Grey Selchie of Sule Skerrie

In Norway land there lived a maid,
"Hush bee loo lillie" this maid began;
"I know not where my baby's father is,
Whether by land or sea he does travel in."

It happened on a certain day
When this fair lady fell fast asleep,
That in cam' a good greay selchie
And set him down at her bed feet,

Sayin' "Awak, awak, my pretty maid,
For oh, how sound as thou dost sleep!
An' I'll tell thee where thy baby's father is —
He's sittin' close at thy bed feet!"

"I pray, come tell to me thy name,
Oh, tell me where does thy dwelling be?"
"My name it is good Hein Mailer
An' I earn my livin' oot o' the sea.

I am a man upo' the land,
I am a selchie in the sea,
And when I'm far frae every strand
My dwellin' is in Sule Skerrie."

"Alas, alas, this woeful fate! —
  This weary fate that's been laid for me,
  That a man should come from the Wast o' Hoy
  To the Norway lands to have a bairn wi' me!"

"My dear, I'll wed thee with a ring,
  With a ring, my dear, I'll wed with thee."
"Thoo may go wed thee weddens wi' whom thoo wilt,
  For I'm sure thoo'll never wed none wi' me!"

"Thoo wilt nurse my little wee son
  For seven long years upo' thy knee,
  An' at the end o' seven long years
  I'll come back and pay the norish fee."

Now he had ta'en a purse of guld
  And he has put it upon her knee,
  Sayin' "Gi'e to me my little young son,
  An' take thee up thy nourrice fee."

She says "My dear, I'll wed thee wi' a ring,
  Wi' a ring, my dear, I'll wed wi' thee!"
"Thoo may go wed these [thee's] weddens wi' whom
    thoo wilt,
  For I'm sure thoo'll never wed none wi' me!

But I'll put a gold chain round his neck
  An' a gey good gold chain it'll be,
  That if ever he comes to the Norway lands
  Thoo may have a gey good guess on he,

An' thoo will get a gunner good,
  An' a gey good gunner it will be,
  An' he'll gae oot on a May mornin'
  An' shoot the son an' the grey selchie."

Oh, she has got a gunner good,
  An' a gey good gunner it was he,

An' he went out on a May mornin'
An' he shot the son an' the grey selchie.

When the gunner returned from his expedition he showed the
Norway woman the gold chain he had found round the neck of a
young seal, and a final verse expresses her grief:

"Alas, alas this woeful fate
This weary fate that's been laid for me."
And once or twice she sobbed an' sighed,
An' her tender heart did brak' in three.

In 1859 the minister of North Ronaldsay, Orkney, sent to John
Campbell of Islay another version of this ballad. It is among Campbell's unpublished manuscripts.

Sealchie Sang

I heard a Mither baing her bairn
An' ay she rockit an' she sang
She took sae hard upo' the verse
Till the heart within her body rang

"O row cradle an' go cradle
An' ay sleep thon my bairn within
O little ken I my bairn's faither
Or yet the land that he liggs in"

O up then spake a grimly Ghost
A aye sae laigh at her bed's feet
"O here am I thy bairns faither
Although I'm nae thy luve sae sweet

Jo Immrannoe it is my name
Jo Immrannoe they do ca' me
An' my lands they lie baith braid an' wide
Amang the rocks o' Sule Skerry

An' foster weel my young young son
An' for a twalmont an a day
An' when the twalmonts fairly done
I'll come an' pay the nourice's fee"

"But how shall I my young son ken
An' how shall I my young son know?"
" 'Mang a' the Selkies i' Sule Skerry
He will be midmost amang them a' "

"My husband is a proud gunner
An' aye a proud gunner is he
An' the first shot that he will fire
Will be at my young son an' thee"

"I fear nee livin' proud gunner
I fear nee mortal man" quo he
"For pouther winna burn i' saut
Sae I an' thy young Son'll gee free"

O when that weary twalmont geed
He cam to pay the nourice fee
He had ae coffer fu' o' gowd
An' anither fu' o' white money

"Upo' the Skerry is thy young son
Upo' the Skerry lieth he
Sin thou wilt see they ain young son
Now is the time to speak wi' he"

The Gunner lay ahind a rock
Ahind a tangie rock lay he
An' the very first shot the gunner loot
It strack his wife aboon the bree

Jo Immrannoe an' his young son
Wi' heavy hearts took tae the sea
Let a' that live on mortal Lird
Ne'er mell wi' Selchies o' the sea

From the Shetland Islands there is yet another version—see *Child's Ballads* and *County Folk-Lore*, Vol. 3 (London, 1903).

Tadhg Murphy (Ó Murchú), of Waterville, County Kerry, in Ireland, was one of the people who told me that seals are fond of music. He says that a good singer can coax them ashore. His great-uncle, the poet Sean òg Murchú, who had a very sweet voice, was walking by the shore one day when he saw a seal sunning herself on the top of the water about fifty yards out. He began to sing to her as one might sing to put a child to sleep: "Come ashore, come ashore, O seal!"

Tadhg says that the song pleased the seal so much that she fell "dead asleep on the top of the water." The waves were rocking her and, although the tide was ebbing, she kept on coming in and coming in until she was lying high and dry, and asleep, on the sand.

Tadhg was unable to remember the tune to which the words were sung, but Francis Collinson, of Edinburgh University, has shown me some music used for the same purpose in Scotland. It is Number 46 in Patrick MacDonald's *Collection of Highland Vocal Airs hitherto unpublished* (Edinburgh, 1784).

The Fisherman's Song for Attracting the Seals

There was also a belief that the seals themselves could sing. In the introduction to his great book *The Songs of John MacCodrum* (Scottish Gaelic Texts Society: Edinburgh, 1939), William Matheson gives some words of a lament which was sung by a seal somewhere near the island of North Uist in the days when the flesh of seals was commonly eaten. MacCodrum used the air for his "Smeorach Chlann Domhnaill," but he altered the chorus to suit the notes of the mavis. Mr. Matheson has kindly given me the tune as he himself has heard it sung to the older song.

Hó i Hó i

Here is a literal translation. The opening sounds have no meaning.

> Hó i hó i hi o hó i
> Hó i hi o hó ìi
> Hó i hó i hi o hó i
> Last night I was not alone.
>
> It is a pity that in this land
> They eat human beings in the form of food.
> Do you not see the leader of the Seal Host
> Boiling fiercely on a fire?
>
> Hó i hó etc.,
> Last night I was not alone.
>
> I am the daughter of Hugh the son of Owen.
> I know the skerries well.
> Woe betide the person who would strike me
> For I am a gentlewoman from another land.

On page 15 of *Songs of the Hebrides*, Volume 1 (London, 1909),
Kenneth MacLeod has a note on "The Seal-woman's Croon."

The seals are the children of the King of Lochlann under spells—
clann Righ Lochlainn fo gheasaibh. Beauty, wisdom, and bravery
were in their blood as well as in their skins, and that was why their
step-mother took the hate of destruction for them, and live she
would not unless she got them out of the way. Seven long years
did she spend with a namely magician, a-learning of the Black Art,
until at last she was as good as her master at it, with a woman's wit
forby. And what think ye of it!—did not the terrible carlin put her
step-children under eternal spells, that they should be half-fish
half-beast so long as waves should beat on the shores of Lochlann!
Och! Och! that was the black deed—sure you would know by the
very eyes of the seals that there is kingly blood in them. But the
worst is still untold. Three times in the year, when the full moon
is brightest, the seals must go back to their own natural state,
whether they wish it or no. Their step-mother put this in the spells

so that there might be a world of envy and sorrow in their hearts every time they saw others ruling in the kingdom which is theirs by right of blood. And if you were to see one of them as they should be always, if right were kept, you would take the love of your heart for that one, and if weddings were in your thoughts, sure enough a wedding there would be. Long ago, and not so long ago either, a man in Canna was shore-wandering on an autumn night and the moon full, and did he not see one of the seal lady-lords washing herself in a streamlet that was meeting the waves! And just as I said, he took the love of his heart for her, and he went and put deep sleep on her with a sort of charm that he had, and he carried her home in his arms. But och! och! when the wakening came, what had he before him but a seal! And though he needed all the goodness he had, love put softening in his heart, and he carried her down to the sea and let her swim away to her own kith and kin, where she ought to be. And she spent that night, it is said, on a reef near the shore, singing like a daft mavis, and this is one of her croons—indeed, all the seals are good at the songs, and though they are really of the race of Lochlann, it is the Gaelic they like best.

The Seal-woman's Croon

Bheir mi hiù― ra bho nail-e bho___ Bheir mi hiù― ra bho ho ro i___ Bheir mi hiù_ ro bho nail-e bho__ An ca-dal trom___ 's an dea-chaidh mi.

The only words here which have any meaning are "An cadal trom 's an deachaidh mi"—the deep sleep into which I went.

In Volume 2 of the same book (p.146), Kenneth MacLeod says:

The Islesman in whom goodness is stronger than love, finding the sealwoman bathing in the creek, will let her go back to her own natural element; the Islesman in whom love is stronger than goodness cunningly hides her skin, and weds her on the third night after he has found her.

The sealwoman was hot and tired baking the bread and making the churn against her husband's return from the hunting-hill. 'Ochón, the burning of me,' thought she, 'what would I not give for a dive and a dip into the beauteous coolness of the cool sea-water!' On the very heel of her words, who rushed in but her wee laddie, his two eyes aglow. 'O mother, mother,' cried he, 'is not this the strange thing I have found in the old barley-kist, a thing softer than mist to my touch!' And if she looked, and look she did, this strange thing, softer than mist, was it not her own skin! Quickly, deftly, the sealwoman, tired and hot, put it on, and taking the straight track to the shore, it was nought for her then but a dip down and a keek up, all evening long, in the beauteous coolness of the cool sea-water. 'Wee laddie of my heart,' said she, ere night came upon her, 'when thou and thy father will be in want, thou wilt set thy net off this rock, and thy mother will throw into it the choice fish that will make a laddie grow, and a man pleased with himself.'

And the sealwoman, with a dip down and a keek up, went lilting her sea-joy in the cool sea-water.

The Seal-woman's Sea Joy

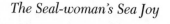

Ionn   da   ionn   do   Ionn   da

Fine   Repeat 3 times   *D. C.*

od-ar   da.   Hi-o-dan dao   od-ar   da.

It was by singing this melody that Marjory Kennedy-Fraser attracted the attention of some seals when she was on the island of Barra. She describes her experience in the introduction to her book *From the Hebrides* (Glasgow, 1925):

> As I was returning by the western shore from my second visit to North Bay, I chanced on two of my friends, the 'cellist whom I have already mentioned and her sister, a violinist, resting on the sands in the warm afternoon sun. Glad of the rest, I lay down between them on the sands. We were some little distance from the water's edge, parallel with which out in the sea, ran a long line of skerries, reefs that are covered at high tide. On the skerries were stretched, also basking in the sunlight, innumerable great grey seals, seals that visit these isles only at long intervals. My friends, great enthusiasts for Hebridean songs, who use their own string instrument arrangements of them for their students, said to me: 'Try singing "The Sealwoman's Sea-joy" to the seals themselves.' I raised myself on my elbow—I was too lazily happy at the moment to stand erect—and, with the most carrying tone I could summon, sang the first phrase of the song. Instantly the response began at the southern end of the reef, and a perfect fusillade of single answering tones came from seal after seal, travelling rapidly northward, until at the further end of the reef it ceased. Then, after a moment of intense silence, a beautiful solo voice sang this phrase:

Adagio Cantabile

The voice was quite human in character but much greater in volume than any mezzo-soprano I have ever heard.

Is the song I sang really a seal song, and did the Isles folk learn it from the seals? I noted it many years ago from an old Uist woman. Did the seals mistake me for one of themselves, and had the phrase I sang a meaning for them, and did they instantly grasp it and answer it?

In their answering phrase the solo seal sang the interval of an ascending sixth, a favourite melodic step with the Isles folk in their tunes. Did the Isles folk borrow this of the seals or the seals of the Isles folk?

That these seals knew the whole of my tune, although I had sung only half of it to them, appeared when later in the same month and year, my friends discovered them singing the second half.

Was singing perhaps the earliest form of human speech, as Hudson, with his 'Rima', would suggest, and were the Syrens of Greek story and the Lorelei of the North just such pre-human singers?

The sounds made by the seals are in fact so foreign to the ear, and so elusive, that it would be almost impossible to note them accurately on paper after a single hearing at a distance in the open air. Only by using recording gear can one be certain. Thanks to the skill and endurance of Dr. Ludwig Koch, the world's first and greatest expert on recorded sound, there does exist one record of a gray seal singing. By placing his microphone in the caves and on the cliffs and shores of the island of Skomer, he obtained many perfect recordings of the voices of seals at play, in love, in anger, in distress; and during a terrible storm, which wrecked the temporary hut built to protect his gear, he heard through his earphones these notes:

Ludwig Koch's Seal

°This note is rather sharp in pitch.

Francis Collinson transcribed this from Ludwig Koch's disc and contributed it to the *Journal of the English Folk Dance and Song Society* (see Ethel Baisin's article in Vol. 6, No. 3, 1951).

One cannot get a true idea of the phrase by playing it on the piano. The chanter or the fiddle gets nearer to it. Ludwig Koch tells me that he thinks it was sung by a bachelor seal, lonely and disconsolate upon a rock.

Acknowledgments

In one form or another I have myself heard every story in this book, but where the story told to me was incomplete I have borrowed from, or substituted, the best version I can find in printed or manuscript collections of oral tradition. I wish to thank everyone who helped me in this way, among whom are Michael Corduff, Professor J. H. Delargy, Séamus Ennis, Liam Mac Meanman, Brian McLoughlin, Calum Maclean, Tadgh Ó Murchú, Seán Ó Súilleabháin, and Professor Éamonn Ó Tuathail of Trinity College, Dublin.

I am indebted similarly to the following books: *Popular Superstitions and Festive Amusements of the Highlanders of Scotland*, by W. Grant Stewart (Edinburgh, 1823), *Hero-Tales of Ireland*, edited by Jeremiah Curtin (London, 1894), and *County Folk-Lore*, Volume 3 (Orkney and Shetland Islands), by George F. Black (London, 1903).

I think I remembered to mention Lord Chesterfield and everybody else as I went along.

About the Author

David Robert Alexander Thomson was born in India of Scottish parents in 1914. His father had served in the Indian Army for a number of years before being badly wounded in the trenches of Europe. On returning to Britain the family stayed with David's grandparents in Nairn, a fishing town by the Moray Firth; they later moved to Derbyshire and then to London. At the age of eleven he sustained an eye injury that made school impossible for him and impaired his vision for the rest of his life. To aid recovery he was sent to stay with his mother's mother in Nairn and was taught by private tutors. The memories of these formative years in Scotland went into his final book, *Nairn in Darkness and Light*, which was awarded the McVitie's Scottish Book Prize for 1987 and, posthumously, the first NCR Book Award for Nonfiction.

Allowed back to school at the age of fourteen, Thomson went to King Alfred's in London and on to Lincoln College at Oxford to read modern history. During vacations and after graduating in 1936 he took tutoring jobs. He spent nearly a decade as private tutor to the Kirkwoods, an Anglo-Irish family in County Roscommon, and wrote memorably of his Irish experience in *Woodbrook* (1974).

In 1943 Thomson joined the BBC, where he worked for the next twenty-six years as a writer and producer of radio documentaries. He made many distinguished programs, including a series called "The Irish Storyteller," a series on animal folklore, and "The Great

Hunger," about the Irish famine of 1845–48. Thomson's love of the natural world, rural communities and oral traditions came together in his first book, *The People of the Sea*. In 1972 he published a similar book, *The Leaping Hare*, with the folklorist George Ewart Evans.

In 1953–54 Thomson was seconded to UNESCO as a writer-producer making radio programs in France, Liberia and Turkey. He met his wife, Martina, in 1952, and his book *In Camden Town* (1983) is a record, in the form of a diary, of the community in which they made their home after 1956. He published three novels, *Daniel* (1962), *Break in the Sun* (1965) and *Dandiprat's Days* (1983), as well as the much-loved children's books about Danny Fox. His abiding interest in Irish life found further expression in his edition of the diaries of Elizabeth Smith of Rothiemurchus, a firsthand account of the Great Hunger.

David Thomson died in London, in February 1988.